"Sprouted whole grain flour baked goods taste so much better than those using white flour. It is better for me and I feel better. I have been eating sprouted flour baked goods for more than two years and I won't ever go back to those made with white flour. It also makes me feel good that I am doing something good for my family." —M. CONKLIN

"Sprouted whole grain flour is so healthy: more nutrition, more fiber, more flavor!" —K. ELDERMAN

"It is hard to find a treat that isn't full of bad stuff like bleached flour, processed sugar, and fat. Thanks to the recipes from Essential Eating, I can enjoy healthy cookies, pastries, and my own biscotti made with sprouted flour without feeling I have started the day on the wrong foot." —C. BURNS

"Sprouted whole grain flour fills me up, and tastes YUMMY!" —P. DAVIDSON

"I don't get constipated from sprouted breads and flours!! I can't believe I just said that." —J. KALIN

"My children just love the sprouted waffles! They thought I was baking cookies but I was using the waffle iron! I make them in a big batch and freeze them so they can have sprouted waffles before school!" —C. MASSARO

"Now I only eat bread that is made with sprouted whole grain flour. After eliminating white and whole grain flour from my diet, my body became more regular and I began losing weight effortlessly. Now I don't have the inflammation in my digestive tract that I had from eating white flour." —C. BALLARD

"I believe sprouted whole grain flour is truly the way food was intended to taste—flavorful, wholesome, delicious and nurturing." —M. JEFFREY

ESSENTIAL EATING
Sprouted Baking
with whole grain flours that digest as vegetables

JANIE QUINN

Award-winning author,
Essential Eating The Digestible Diet

AZURE MOON PUBLISHING
Waverly, Pennsylvania
www.essentialliving.com   EssentialEating.com

Essential Eating Sprouted Baking
with whole grain flours that digest as vegetables

Published by Azure Moon Publishing
Post Office Box 771, Waverly, PA 18471
(570) 586–1557

For information or additional books:
www.EssentialEating.com

Managing Editor: Yvonne Eckman
Editor: Lee Ann Cavanaugh
Recipe Editor: Rebekah Gillette
Photography: Kathryn Lesoine, Stone Road Studios
Book Design: Cindy Szili, North Market Street Graphics
Illustrations: ZebraZio Media

Library of Congress Cataloging-in-Publication Data is available
Library of Congress Control Number: 2008928998
ISBN: 978-0-967-98433-9

Printed in the United States on acid-free 100% recyclable sustainable-forested paper with vegetable-based ink

sprout·ed whole grain flour (sprout·ed hōl grān flour) *n.*

a fine, powdery vegetable foodstuff obtained by milling seeds of grain (grass) that have germinated into living plants; made from the entire grain including the bran, germ and endosperm; a nutrient-dense source of nourishment

Producing a high-quality sprouted flour requires that the sprouting and milling process be precisely monitored and accurately measured to assure a high sprout content. Refer to page 13 for details.

Contents

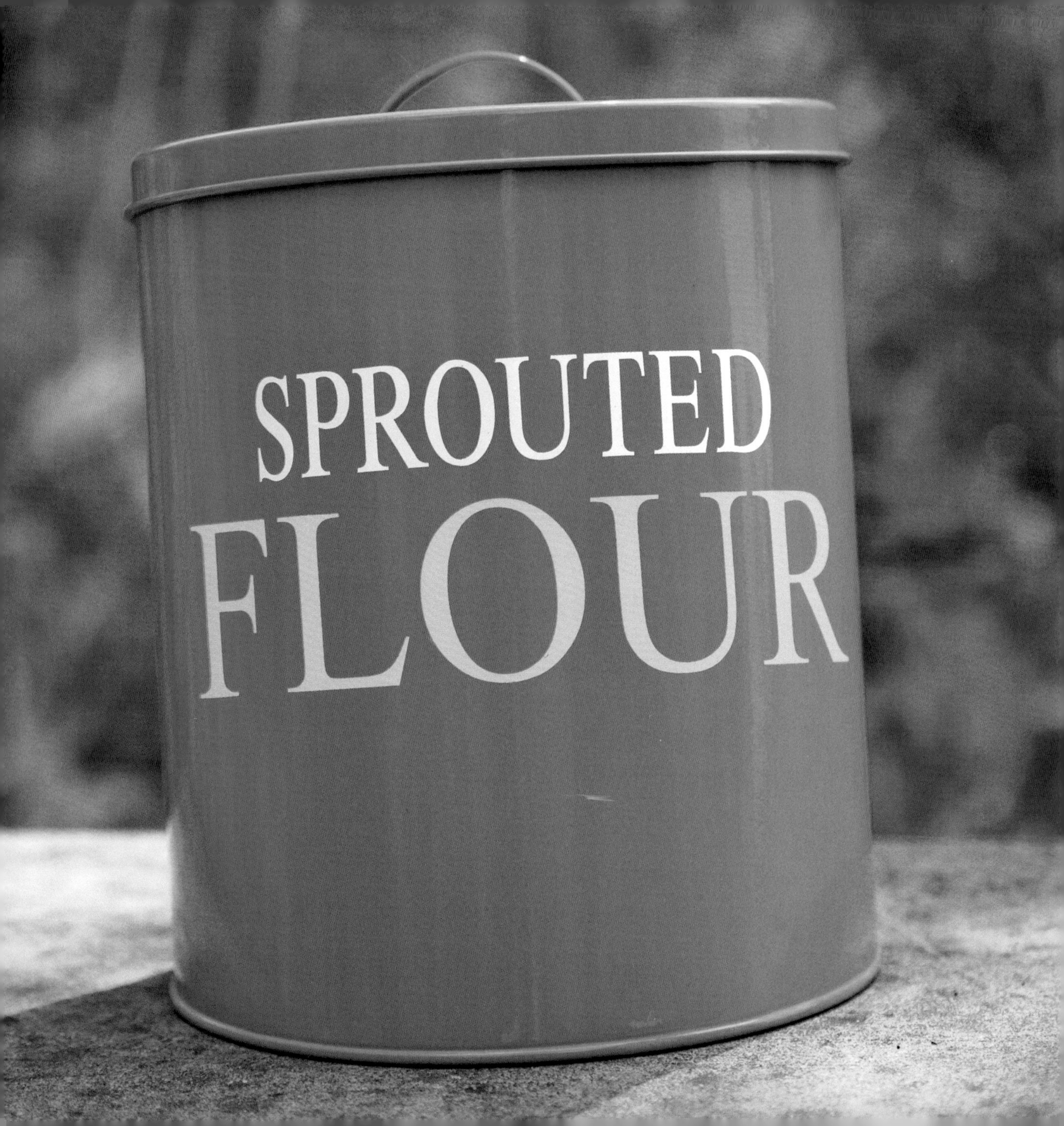
SPROUTED
FLOUR

About This Book

One of the most instrumental factors in restoring my health, losing my excess weight and eliminating my indigestion was discovering that sprouted whole grain flours digest the same as vegetables. Incorporating *sprouted* whole grain baked goods into my diet restored my spirit and allowed me to enjoy the simple yet wonderful pleasure of eating easily digested carbohydrates again. For the past 15 years this one simple fact has changed and enhanced my life and is now the reason and the premise for this book. I am honored to introduce to you the simplicity and the rewards of baking with flour that digests the same as a vegetable.

I had begun to bake with sprouted flour out of necessity. I now continue to bake with it out of a natural desire—the desire to enjoy an amazing variety of foods that support my health and allow me to experience the joy of living in a healthy body. When I realized how great "feeling good" felt, the decision to continue baking with sprouted flour was very easy.

This book shows both experienced and novice bakers the beauty and the benefits of incorporating delicious sprouted whole grain flour into their diets. Imagine eating a cookie made with flour that digests as a vegetable. Now imagine that cookie being the best-tasting cookie you have ever eaten. Contrary to the modern perception, you *can* bake, and it can be very easy. Try it. You are worth it.

This book is about the beauty and magnificent benefits of baking with sprouted flours. Understandably, little has been written about sprouted grains because the focus of the milling and baking industries has been on unsprouted grains for so long. More about this later.

Years ago Peter Eckman, an accomplished manufacturer, Richard Brandt, a milling engineer, and I joined forces to produce sprouted flour—the very best possible. We have pioneered the sprouting process, and our research and resulting discovery have begun to revolutionize the milling and baking industries, returning taste *and* nutrition to flour.

After several years of trial and error and testing and tasting, we assure you that the Essential Eating Spouted Whole Grain Flours are unsurpassed in the industry. We provide sprouted flours that are superior in their consistency, safety and stability. Our goal is to guarantee that the Essential Eating Sprouted Whole Grain Flours remain far superior to any flour that has ever been milled, known or tasted. And best of all, they are available to you. We offer this introductory baking guide along with these simple recipes to enable you to incorporate sprouted flour into your diet and lifestyle.

Thousands of Essential Eaters around the country have replaced refined white flour in their diets with sprouted whole grain flour, which has allowed them to restore their health and lose their excess weight. By making better food choices, they have joined a cultural movement that is improving the landscape of the food world. I invite you to join in and improve the way you eat and feel by discovering the beauty and the benefits of sprouted whole grain flour. It is a delicious and great alternative to refined white flour.

Why deny yourself the enjoyment of a few healthy carbohydrates—especially when they digest as easily as vegetables? Go ahead, bake a few treats such as sprouted cookies, sprouted pancakes or sprouted pizza and experience the ripple effect that starts to improve your health. So dust off your jellyroll pan, grab your sprouted whole grain flour and preheat your oven. This adventure is worthy of your exploration. Start by saving yourself first. You matter.

Essential Eating

ease. Imagine all the extra energy your body will gain simply from eating foods that are easy for your body to process.

Doctors and health-care practitioners agree that we need to get more whole fruits and vegetables into our diets. Knowing that sprouted flour digests as a vegetable and not a starch makes getting more vegetables into your diet much easier. Eating real whole foods is one of the best things you can do for your own health and the health of our planet. Sustainable real food is food that is free of additives such as chemicals, flavorings, colorings, preservatives and pesticides and is not genetically modified, overly processed or irradiated. Essential Eating's sprouted whole grain flour is real food. Food is the foundation for your health, and your health affects everything and everyone in your life. Essential Eating offers you a path to experiencing the joy of living in a healthy body. The pleasure will be yours.

Sprouted Flour

The Evolution and Milling
of Sprouted Flour

Many indigenous cultures knew the benefits of soaking and sprouting dried grains for better digestion and mineral absorption. They used techniques that had been handed down for generations to germinate grains to produce a more beneficial food. Although indigenous cultures did not have the benefit of the scientific knowledge we possess today, they innately understood that sprouting grains made them easier to digest. Over time these customs and techniques for sprouting grains were lost, so modern food production did not employ them.

In the absence of modern machinery prior to the 1900s, grain was harvested by hand and stored in the field. While stored, the grain would partially sprout as it soaked up moisture from precipitation. Although the grain sprouted naturally in the field, the process was not able to be controlled, and the grain would usually lose its integrity by the time it was milled. Grain that had sprouted naturally in the field also had the potential to mold easily, resulting in flour that was unacceptable for baking. Thus, grain that was stored this way was considered damaged goods. It was a volatile organic commodity that presented problems in milling because it lacked consistency and contained undesirable bacteria and pestilent growth.

The introduction of the combine harvester in the early 1900s significantly changed the milling industry and assisted in reducing the problem of sprout damage. It allowed grain to be harvested from the field and transported directly to storage bins. Since the grain was no longer exposed to moisture, it was less likely to sprout. The focus in milling shifted to preventing sprout damage and stabilizing grain to produce flour that was more easily manufactured and marketed, but not more nutritious. That remains the focus today.

The varieties of grains and the number of mills have been dwindling for many years because of innovations in milling. Over 200 years ago, there were more than 22,000 mills in the United States, which had a population of about 5.3 million people at that time. Today there are about 190 mills, with a population of about 300 million people. What happened? Grain and flour suspended in a dry, unsprouted state proved easier to preserve, manufacture, transport and store. Milling became a completely controlled dry operation, extending the shelf life of white flour and allowing for longer transportation distances so that fewer mills were required to feed more people.

History is being made in milling once again with the recent introduction of the Essential Eating Sprouted Whole Grain Flours. Unlike grains that sprouted accidentally in the field,

resulting in a low-quality flour, a specific controlled sprouting and milling technology is now being used to produce this type of flour. This technology allows the sprout to develop, then be stabilized, capturing the sprout at its peak. The sprout is then rinsed and dried to ensure integrity. This method captures the natural wonders of the grain while maintaining its nutritional value and quality, ushering in a new generation of healthy flours.

Years ago, in a continued effort to stabilize grain for mass production and in response to commercial baking requirements,

modern milling stripped the fiber and vital nutrients from the grain. Grains that had once been full of fiber and nutrient-rich, constituting an important component of our diet, were now "refined" and nutrient-deficient. White flour was born. One baker dismissed it as "air-whipped wheat candy." Another baker commented, "We use refined white flour to make the bread look good, but we don't count on it for any taste or nutritional benefit." Unsprouted, stable, refined white flour that has been stripped of fiber and nutrients and then re-enriched with manufactured nutrients has become the mainstay of commercial baking. It is one of the most consumed food ingredients in America.

The effect of modern commercial baking is reflected in the decline of our nation's health. Refined, unsprouted white flour has been linked to the escalation of serious illness in America. Whole grain flour contains more fiber and more nutrients than refined white flour, but it cannot be compared to or substituted for the nutritional and digestive benefits of sprouted whole grain flour. Sprouted whole grain flour is milled from a plant, not a seed, and therefore is easier for the body to process. The reintroduction of sprouted whole grain flour will likely play a large part in the treatment and prevention of serious dis-eases such as heart disease, cancer and diabetes, all of which are occurring with increasing frequency in today's society.

The process of milling grain plays an important part in the end product we call flour. For thousands of years, the only option for producing flour was to grind grain using a mill-

stone. During the milling process, the surface of the stone would be ground down as well, and this ground stone went directly into the flour. The miller also had to pay close attention that the stone did not become overheated and scorch the flour. Stone grinding is not the most efficient, sanitary, unprocessed or low-temperature way to mill flour, and by the early 1960s most facilities had converted to more efficient steel roller mill systems, which offered better quality control.

As this modern technology replaced the old stone mills, the term *stone-ground,* as applied to flour, became a marketing tool. Because the Food and Drug Administration (FDA) does not regulate use of the term, it can be used indiscriminately. Like other such terms—*natural, homemade* and *healthy,* for example—describing flour as *stone-ground* is considered puffery on many food labels.

The certified organic Essential Eating Sprouted Whole Grain Flours are milled using a modern, sanitary, lower-temperature milling system to produce a superior-quality, safe, nutritious flour. Our philosophy of milling sprouted whole grains is based on restoration and preservation, not the current mind-set of flour production that relies mainly on extracting and then enriching.

As with other real whole foods, all sprouted flours and their products are not created equal. The fact that the word *sprouted* is not regulated certainly makes us question how much of a particular food making that claim is actually sprouted. Essential Eating Sprouted Foods has spent years on research and development to test for and maintain the highest percentage of sprout in their flours as compared with any other sprouted flour or sprouted products.

The falling number test is used in traditional milling to determine whether a grain has sprout damage. In *sprouted* milling, the falling number test is used to determine how much sprout a grain has achieved. These are two very different reasons for the same test. In traditional milling, the desired test result is a high falling number, which usually indicates low enzyme activity. In sprouted milling, a lower falling number is preferable, indicating a high level of enzyme activity. It is important to note that the falling number prior to sprouting compared to the falling number after sprouting is an accurate measure of how much sprout action has occurred. A grain that started with a falling number of 350 and is now at 150 has sprouted more completely than a grain that started at 250 and is now at 150. To ensure that Essential Eating Sprouted Whole Grain Flours contain the highest level of sprout action, the final falling number must always be equal to or lower than half of the falling number prior to sprouting. Superior grain that has been sprouted and stabilized, resulting in a low falling number, is very difficult to achieve. The Essential Eating Sprouted Whole Grain Flours have realized this level of excellence.

There is a huge difference between true sprouted flour products and mash products, which are usually referred to as *flourless* or *manna*. Bread products made from a mash are created by mixing wet sprouts that have been wet-milled or soaked with water to form the dough. These wet-milled sprouted products skip the drying, sifting and milling process, which are important steps in ensur-

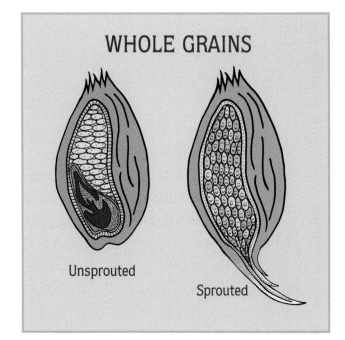

WHOLE GRAINS

Unsprouted

Sprouted

ing the safety and quality of the end product. Therefore, in the wet-milling process, there is potential for foreign matter to remain in the mash. Furthermore, there is a distinction between soaking the grain and sprouting it. Grain may appear to the naked eye to be sprouted when it has actually been drowned, resulting in the swollen endosperm pushing through the bran coat. In short, drowned grain does not possess the benefits derived from sprouting. Sprouted products made from a mash are much coarser in texture and can have a distinctive fermented taste. Now that I have experienced the taste and texture of products made with sprouted flour and understand the manufacturing process, I choose not to eat mash or manna breads made from wet sprouts.

There is also a major difference between the familiar sprouts that are available in grocery stores and the sprouting process we are discussing here. The former are mature sprouts that have been grown for approximately seven days into leggy green shoots. On the other hand, the process for sprouting a grain used in sprouted flour is much shorter and does not produce a sprout with a green shoot; this short sprout is immediately dried prior to milling.

The recent warnings about bacterial risks from eating sprouts concern mature raw legume sprouts, which are different from the sprout used for this flour. The Essential Eating Sprouted Whole Grain Flour is not made from raw sprouts, but from grains that have been sprouted and then dried to the degree required to maximize their nutritional benefits.

The mission of Essential Eating Sprouted Foods is to provide organic, nutritious and sustainable sprouted flour and food products. This company represents small-scale quality food production, artisan processing and creative distribution chains. Bringing this beneficial food into neighborhoods has been a labor of love. The future of our food supply depends on such innovative operations. This book celebrates sprouted whole grain flour—a real whole food that can become a staple in our American diet. Delicious sprouted flour breads and baked goods are currently being made and consumed with pleasure. Bakers are awakening to the realization that healthy flour is available, and the results speak for themselves!

The Beauty and the Benefits of Sprouted Flour

The beauty of sprouted whole grain flour is that it makes available more vital nutrients than unsprouted flour. The major benefit is that those nutrients are in a state that can more readily be absorbed and digested by the body.

Grains are seeds. Unsprouted seeds hold the nutrients, vitamins and minerals in a dormant state. The germ portion of the seed contains all the genetic information to turn that seed into a full-grown plant, as well as the enzymes necessary for sprouting. When the grain cell germinates, or sprouts, that genetic information ignites, and the resulting amylase activity, or enzymatic action, ultimately results in plant growth. During the sprouting process, the starch molecules, or complex carbohydrates, are broken down into smaller parts, referred to as simple sugars. Simple sugars are the building blocks that make up complex carbohydrates but in a form that the body absorbs more easily. The body recognizes and readily digests simple sugars for quick energy, as opposed to starches that can be stored as fat. The grain sprouts, transforming itself into a plant, and we know that plants consist primarily of simple sugars that easily digest in the body in the form of vegetables.

Who says sprouted grains are a vegetable? In 2008 the USDA's Food Safety and Inspection Service (FSIS) ruled that sprouted grains are more akin to vegetables than to whole grains. The Whole Grain Council partnered with the American Association of Cereal Chemists (AACC) International's Whole Grains Task Force to formulate the following statement that was issued by AACC International's Board of Directors: "Sprouted grains containing all of the original bran, germ and endosperm shall be considered whole grains as long as the sprout growth does not exceed kernel length and nutrient values have not diminished." The USDA/FSIS revised its earlier ruling and now allows sprouted whole grains to be considered as whole grains. What I find interesting is the absence of an American Association of Vegetable Chemists! Who is defending the classification of whole grains as vegetables?

Unsprouted whole grains are storage cells. The whole kernel of grain stores vital nutrients that are not in a form that the body can absorb as well as when the grain is sprouted. Milling unsprouted whole grains merely grinds the storage cell. No matter how fine or coarse the grind, it remains in the completely unsprouted dried seed state. Grinding or milling a whole grain does not change its properties. However, sprouting does!

Sprouting naturally manufactures vitamin C, increases vitamin B content and carotene levels and aids the body's absorption of calcium, magnesium, iron, copper and zinc. The nutritional components of sprouting are succinctly explained by Sally Fallon, author of *Nourishing Traditions* (New Trends Publishing, 1999) and president of the Weston

A. Price Foundation. Phytic acid, an organic acid in which phosphorus is bound, is present in the outer, or bran, layer of whole grain. Phytic acid, an enzyme inhibitor, can combine with calcium, magnesium, copper, iron and especially zinc in the intestinal tract and block their absorption. Sprouted grains contain enzymes, lactobacilli and other helpful organisms that break down and neutralize phytic acid, allowing the body to better absorb the nutrients. The enzyme activity and lactobacilli growth that occurs when grains sprout therefore aid in digestion.

The University of Minnesota reported that sprouted whole wheat was found to have 28 percent more thiamine (vitamin B_1), 315 percent more riboflavin (vitamin B_2), 66 percent more niacin (vitamin B_3), 65 percent more pantothenic acid (vitamin B_5), 111 percent more biotin, 278 percent more folic acid and 300 percent more vitamin C in comparison with unsprouted whole wheat.

Everyone wants to know how sprouted whole grain flours taste. Whole wheat baked goods have a reputation for tasting bitter, even though most contain only a small percentage of whole grains. The sprouting process results in amazingly tasty flour that is mild and full of flavor, with no bitterness. The most frequent comment from our students at the Essential Eating Lifestyle and Cooking School is "This is delicious," which always makes me laugh—isn't food supposed to taste good? Flavor rules! Organic baked goods made with sprouted flour are some of the best-tasting foods you will ever eat because the authentic flavor of the grain has been allowed to develop, yielding a real, whole, digestible food. One student ironically exclaimed, "This tastes too good to be healthy!"

People who have begun eating sprouted whole grain baked goods have reported results that range from excess weight melting off to bowel regularity. Additional benefits cited include lower cholesterol, more energy, less arthritis pain, controlled blood pressure, improved digestion and sounder sleep. Interestingly enough, bowel regularity, and the quality-of-life enhancement that accompanies it, tops the list of issues resolved by switching to sprouted foods. This is not surprising once you recognize that sprouted flour digests as easily as vegetables, a fibrous food group that most American diets lack.

As with anything that is good for you, sprouted food can have adverse effects when indulged in to excess. Because sprouted whole grain flour is such a potent, nutrient-dense food, eating too much of it may overstimulate the colon. Consuming this food in moderate quantities, such as a couple slices of bread, a muffin or a few cookies, contributes to healthy digestion and elimination. Listen to your body; it is a marvelously smart machine.

You can now enjoy breads and other products made with sprouted whole grain flour that is easy for the body to process. Your eating lifestyle can even include your favorite comfort foods, like bread, pasta and pizza. The benefits are numerous, and the results are satisfying and lasting. Sprouted whole grain flour is becoming a delicious alternative to white flour in our culture, and ongoing research continues to discover additional beneficial properties of sprouted grains.

Gluten and Types of Flour

Gluten is the general name given to the protein present in grain. The gluten content varies widely among the three most popular types of flour. *Durum flour* has the highest protein, or gluten, content and is used for pasta products. *Hard flour* has the next-highest protein content and is used for leavened baked goods such as breads, rolls, pizza dough and bagels. *Soft flour* contains the lowest amount of protein and is used for unleavened baked goods such as pastry, cakes, cookies and pretzels. All three types of flour can be milled in white or whole grain forms. *All-purpose flour,* a subclass of hard flour, has a medium protein level and can be used to make most leavened and pastry baked goods. *Spelt flour* is similar to soft flour, in that it does not possess optimum leavening ability.

It is possible to produce most types of flour from sprouted whole grains with spectacular results. There are two sprouted flours currently available to consumers: sprouted whole wheat and sprouted whole spelt. Essential Eating Sprouted Whole Grain Flours are also being milled for commercial bakers who are producing sprouted whole grain products and delivering them to markets as this book is being written.

The recipes in this book can be made with either Essential Eating Sprouted Whole Wheat or Sprouted Whole Spelt Flour. For best results, use the sprouted whole wheat flour for leavened goods and those needing more protein, such as bread, pizza, bagels and pasta. Use Sprouted Whole Grain Spelt for unleavened goods, such as muffins, cakes, pastries, cookies and pretzels.

Essential Eating Sprouted Whole Grain Flours are made from the entire grain, including the bran, endosperm and germ. The bran coat, removed in milling white flour, contains virtually all the fiber, vitamins and trace minerals of the grain. The challenge in using whole grain flour for baking, whether it is sprouted or unsprouted, is that the fiber has few baking characteristics. Refined cake and pastry flours have had the germ and bran removed in an effort to make the flour perform better and to achieve a more cosmetically pleasing baking result. Recognizing that sprouted whole grain that includes the bran coat results in a more nutritious and flavorful food item, the recipes in this book have been adapted to make delicious and aesthetically satisfying baked goods with sprouted flours in your home kitchen.

In recent years, whole grain spelt has become more popular. Spelt is an ancient and distant cousin of modern wheat. Spelt is unique in that it has a tough outer hull that must be removed prior to milling. The recent popularity of spelt can most likely be attributed to the fact that, being a different grain, it offers an alternative to those who are wheat-intolerant. In addition, the protein in spelt has a unique combination of amino acids among grains, which may also be a factor in its digestibility.

Gluten, as a protein, is found in grains and other plants. Most people find it easy to digest, but when a body cannot properly digest gluten, serious health issues can result. Although lower in gluten than wheat, spelt nevertheless contains some gluten. For those who are completely gluten-intolerant, any amount, including that in sprouted flour, may still pose a problem. Sprouting alters the gluten in both wheat and spelt, so most starch- and some gluten-sensitive individuals are able to enjoy sprouted flour, but be cautious when introducing this food into your diet if you are gluten-intolerant. Do not despair, however. Many of our students were initially diagnosed with starch sensitivities, yet, after embracing the Essential Eating philosophy and spending some time cleansing their system from a starch-based diet, they found they could digest, without difficulty, sprouted flour products.

Sprouted Baking

The Simple Act of Baking

Let me repeat: You *can* bake and it *is* easy. Without a doubt, you are worth the effort! Baking is a great deal easier than you might think or have been led to believe. Food marketing has convinced us that we do not have the time to make our own meals, bake or even prepare a simple peanut butter and jelly sandwich. Those pre-made PB&J sandwiches in cellophane bags are just screaming at you to succumb to the marketing propaganda that you need them. Contrary to common belief, anyone can bake. It's easy, and the results will be both delicious and nutritious.

The best part about baking at home is the connection you have with the ingredients you are using, which allows you to know what is in your food. Your health and well-being are worth the time you will invest to know what you are ingesting. Making time to bake a few simple sprouted treats means you are less likely to grab for other foods that don't maintain or support your good health. Setting aside a little time to bake can create a sense of peacefulness and slow that fast-lane world to a gentler pace.

The simple act of baking can transform your life. If you are lonely, try whipping up a batch of Carrot Cake Muffins and invite some friends over. If you bake it, they will come. Nothing says you're worth it more than a homemade treat like a warm Cherry Tart. Connect with your kids by baking a Pizza Cookie to tuck into their lunch bags with a note telling them how proud you are of them. Baking is sociable, sensual, sexy and smart. Taking an active part in creating the food that nourishes your body and the bodies of your loved ones is a beautiful thing, a form of grace.

The Sprouted Baking Adventure

This section offers tips for using sprouted flour in your baking. When making a recipe for the first time, it is a good idea not to have any expectations. Relax and regard it as a trial run. The result doesn't have to look like a food magazine cover that has been primped to perfection. As with any first performance, it may not be your best performance, but it will not be your last. The "practice makes perfect" rule applies to baking, too. Every time you make a recipe it will become easier for you. Let's get started.

When baking, it helps to bring liquids and dairy ingredients including eggs, unless otherwise stated, to room temperature before mixing with other ingredients. When called for in a recipe, lukewarm water should be between 105 and 115 degrees Fahrenheit.

When you are creating or using your own recipes, sprouted wheat and sprouted spelt flours may be substituted for all-purpose flour most of the time. As previously mentioned, for best results use sprouted whole wheat flour for leavened recipes such as for bread, pizza dough, bagels and pasta, and sprouted whole spelt flour for unleavened baked goods such as muffins, cakes, cookies, pastries and pretzels. The Essential Eating Sprouted Whole Grain Flours absorb slightly more water than all-purpose flour, so you may need to increase the liquid in your recipe. The Essential Eating Sprouted Whole Grain Flours have less starch damage than traditionally milled flours as a result of the specific milling process. Flour with little starch damage keeps the starch module more intact and allows the dough to absorb more water without turning into a paste, a sign of high-quality flour. Overall, this accounts for less flour being used in the baking process. If you are converting a recipe and the dough is dry, simply add more water or liquids.

The amount of water and the mixing time are crucial elements in baking. Follow the directions for mixing sprouted flour in these recipes. Too little mixing may cause the dough to be crumbly, failing to develop the necessary protein or gluten matrix to expand properly. Too much mixing may break down the protein or gluten. Sprouted flours may require a slightly shorter mixing time, because the gluten is changed and the protein quality has been maximized.

The right amount of water or moisture is necessary for the dough to properly rise. Too little water, and the dough will be dry and dense, trapping the yeast gasses. Too much water, and the baked good may collapse. The proper amount of water develops the protein needed to create structure in baked goods. Even with careful measuring, a few teaspoons' deviance could make the difference in the end result. It is hoped that the first time around, the recipe will perform wonderfully, but when troubleshooting, consider altering the amount of liquid slightly.

Conventional electric ovens, not convection ovens or gas ovens, were used for creating and testing the recipes in this book. Although convection ovens can be far more efficient, as they use fans to circulate the heat, sometimes the air can dry out the baked good faster. When using a convection oven, follow these two guidelines: Set the temperature 50 degrees lower than the recipe calls for, and reduce the baking time by one-fifth to one-quarter. Electric ovens are slightly drier than gas ovens. To add a bit of moisture to an electric oven, use a small baking cup or ramekin filled with hot water, and place it in the oven with the baked good. This might help prevent the crust from forming before the bread has a chance to rise.

Time and temperature are also important. Remember, all ovens are not created equal, and thus temperatures will vary. When making a recipe for the first time, consider setting the timer for five or ten minutes less than the stated baking time. That way, you can test the baked good and extend the time if necessary. Once you determine how long a particular recipe takes to bake in your oven, note it on the recipe for the next time. Test cookies by sight, noting the slight browning at the edges. Test breads by tapping on the bottom of the loaf. The bread is done when the tap sounds hollow. If the tap sounds dense, the bread may need to bake longer. For cakes or muffins, use a sight test to see if the edges have slightly pulled away from the pan or make sure an inserted toothpick comes out clean. You may also lightly touch the surface to see if it is firm and springs back.

When making bread, don't rush the rising time. Most of the flavor develops while bread rises. As a rule, dough has risen sufficiently if you gently press two fingers into it and the indentations spring back slightly or the dough sighs.

Keep in mind that today's wisdom about storing flour is based on grinding unsprouted grains. In an unsprouted grain, the germ, which contains the fat, is still intact. Once milled, that fat begins to degrade over time and may become rancid. During the sprouting process the germ is transformed as the sprout grows, and the molecular structure changes completely, drastically reducing the degradation of the germ when it is milled. Other important factors pertaining to the freshness of flour are the quality of the grain being milled and the way it is cleaned and stored prior to milling. These aspects are key reasons for the superior quality and freshness of Essential Eating Sprouted Whole Grain Flours.

Just as our bodies crave rest after exertion, flour yields better results when it has rested after the milling process. Imagine giving a presentation immediately after running a marathon. Freshly milled flour is stressed—it needs rest! Commercial bakers know that it is hard to obtain optimal results with freshly ground flour, so they often add oxidants and aging agents to shorten the resting time and improve performance. We have found that with proper milling and storing of the sprouted flour, it remains fresh and shelf-stable for much longer than six months. But because we consider sprouted flour a perishable food, for best results consume within six months.

Refrigeration or freezing sprouted flour in an airtight container may extend shelf life. Once exposed to the environment, all food, including flour, begins to oxidize. As stated, oxidized flour actually performs better, as it is ready to take on water and undergo the chemical changes necessary to make dough. Nutrients are not lost through oxidation. Do not store flour near foods or products with strong odors.

Baking is a science, so be accurate when you measure ingredients. It is not necessary to sift sprouted flour, but make sure to scoop flour from the canister and spoon it into the measuring cup, leveling off with a knife for accurate measurement. When measuring wet ingredients, use a glass measuring cup and gauge the amount by viewing the glass at eye level. That way you ensure that the liquid measurement is accurate.

Purchase the very best food ingredients you can find. They will taste better and have more nutrients. The next section further discusses the ingredients used in these recipes.

Ingredients Matter

We are in a time of tremendous change that affords us a tremendous amount of opportunity. The connection has been made between the quality of the food we ingest and the state of our health. Your food dollars are your vote for better-quality food. Locally grown and sustainable foods are good for you and the planet. Buy organic or biodynamic ingredients, especially dairy products. Baking with quality ingredients such as organic sprouted whole grain flour to support your health is a wonderful alternative to the nutritionally deficient products that are abundant. You will find that quality ingredients are worth it.

Reading food labels for ingredients is a good thing, but most often the nutritional information does not tell the true or whole story of a food product. By law, only certain nutrients are required to be listed on labels. A perfect example is unsprouted flour, which has

a nutritional label that is very similar to that for sprouted flour. Nutritional tests used for food labeling do not test for the inherent differences between sprouted and unsprouted grains. Work is under way toward incorporating such testing, but progress is slow, considering the institutions and methods that must be changed in order to make this happen. In the meantime, the labels for these two very different products remain similar. Visit EssentialEating.com for updates on this issue as they develop.

You may also use these easy-to-digest ingredients to convert and create your own recipes. Refer to *Essential Eating The Digestible Diet* and *Essential Eating, A Cookbook* for more recipes and details on digestible foods. See "Sources" at the back of this book for suggested manufacturers of these ingredients.

fruits and vegetables

Fresh or frozen organic fruits are interchangeable in these recipes. **Coconut** is a fruit that can be purchased fresh or dried. Split open the fresh coconut and remove it from the shell. Your grocer would be happy to do the job, or you can do it yourself by striking the shell with a hammer along the midsection while holding it in your hand. Then remove the white meat, peel off the thin brown layer of shell that may remain and grate the meat for recipes. Dried coconut freezes better than fresh coconut. **Cranberries** digest as vegetables. Grocery stores usually carry fresh cranberries from October through January. After that, they are in most frozen foods sections. Dried cranberries may be used in place of raisins, but they tend to be more expensive and have added sugar. **Pumpkin** is great in recipes, especially when you use fresh, but canned is acceptable and convenient. Make sure it is solid-packed, organic pumpkin. **Wild rice** is a grass and therefore digests as a vegetable.

flour and dry ingredients

Substitute **sprouted whole grain flours** for all-purpose flour called for in recipes. **Arrowroot powder,** obtained from the root of a West Indian plant, can be exchanged measure for measure for cornstarch. It is used in recipes requiring a thickener. **Carob powder** comes from the dried bean pods of an evergreen shrub that grows in the Mediterranean. It can be substituted in baking for cocoa powder. Use lightly roasted carob powder, versus raw, as roasting improves the flavor dramatically. Although **carob chips** are sweetened with malted barley and contain oil and an emulsifier (soy lecithin), they are still an easier-to-digest alternative to chocolate chips. **Coconut flour** is a delicious alternative to grain flours for those who desire a gluten-free ingredient. It is high in fiber and has a uniquely natural sweet taste. **Corn flour** is a vegetable that has been ground into flour. **Cornmeal** can be white, yellow or blue in color according to the variety of corn used to produce it. Cornmeal varies in texture from brand to brand. For these recipes, use a finer-ground cornmeal.

Quinoa (pronounced "keen-wa") resembles small grains such as millet or couscous in size and round shape, but it comes from an herb similar to lamb's-quarters. Quinoa does not need to be sprouted to be easily digested. An ancient food referred to as the mother grain of the Inca Indians, quinoa is reappearing as a tasty alternative to wheat. Now grown in North America, quinoa is wheat-free and gluten-free and contains the highest-quality protein of any other grain. The National Academy of Science calls it "one of the best sources of protein in the vegetable kingdom." **Quinoa flour** tastes delicious and may be used for unleavened breads and baked goods such as muffins and pancakes. Use **quinoa flakes** in place of oatmeal in recipes.

Unrefined **sea salt** is a real food that is not altered, nor is iodine added. It is harvested from the ocean and dried by the sun. Celtic Sea Salt is a popular brand. A general rule for weekly consumption is a quarter teaspoon to a half teaspoon of sea salt per person. Your taste buds will adapt as your body comes into balance. An alternative to sea salt is an herb-seasoned salt called **Herbamare.** One of the ingredients in Herbamare is kelp, a sea vegetable with trace iodine. **Tapioca** is extracted and dried from the root of the South American cassava plant. **Tapioca flour** is in a powdered form that bakes beautifully. Being a root vegetable, it easily digests as a vegetable.

sweeteners

Agave nectar, also called **agave syrup,** is a natural sweetener. It is extracted from the heart of the agave cactus plant. Manufactured at a low temperature (less than 118 degrees Fahrenheit), it has a full, sweet flavor with mellow molasses tones. Because it digests slowly in

the body, it prevents spikes in blood sugar. **Date sugar,** made from granulated, dehydrated dates, is sweeter than white sugar and contains more nutrients, especially iron. Three-fourths of a cup of date sugar can be substituted for one cup of maple sugar. **Maple syrup** is a whole food harvested from the sap of a tree. Just like agave nectar, this natural sweetener digests very slowly, also preventing spikes in blood sugar. Always use 100 percent maple syrup and maple products, not syrup substitutes, as they contain fillers and flavorings. Another form of 100 percent maple syrup is **maple sugar,** sometimes called **granulated maple sugar**. It can be used one for one in place of white sugar in recipes. **Powdered maple sugar**, an ultrafine form of maple sugar, is also available. **Maple cream**, sometimes called **maple butter,** is a maple syrup product that has been cooked to a higher temperature, resulting in a thick cream used for icing cakes and cupcakes. Bakers and kids alike have been known to enjoy a spoonful right from the jar to satisfy a craving for sweets. Cooking maple syrup to different consistencies results in the different forms of 100 percent maple syrup sweeteners. The words

malt or *malted* simply indicate that a grain has been fermented or sprouted. Malt, short for *maltose,* refers to the sugar inside the grains. **Barley malt syrup** is boiled until it achieves a dark color and renders a strong, sweet flavor. Sometimes referred to as nondiastatic malt in bread recipes, it adds sweetness and color. We have not used it in these recipes, preferring maple sugar. **Sucanat,** a popular brand of nonrefined granulated cane juice, is a better choice than refined white sugar. It can be substituted in equal measurements for white sugar.

herbs, spices, vanilla and yeast

If a recipe calls for **fresh herbs** and you only have **dried herbs** available, substitute one-third of the required amount of fresh herbs with dried herbs. (In other words, one teaspoon of dried herbs equals one tablespoon of fresh herbs.) Tailor the amount of herbs required in a recipe to suit your palate or sensitivity. Do not wash fresh herbs until you are

ready to use them in a recipe. Fresh herbs can be stored in the refrigerator in a cup with their stems sitting in an inch of water. Have fun experimenting with your favorite herbs in these recipes. Use only organic, fair-trade **vanilla extract**. The recipes with yeast use active-dry or rapid-rise **yeast**.

fats

One-hundred-percent real **butter** is the easiest fat for the body to digest—opt for organic butter. Butter can sometimes burn at high temperatures. If you need to grease a pan for baking, use **ghee,** or clarified butter, from which the milk solids have been removed, making it tolerant of high heat. Cold-pressed, extra-virgin organic **Olive Oil** is the easiest-to-digest concentrated oil. **Coconut oil** has resurfaced as one of the good fats and may be used in place of olive oil in these recipes if you prefer a mild coconut taste. **Vegenaise** is a delicious brand of mayonnaise made with grapeseed oil, which is easier to digest than other concentrated oils.

dairy foods

Eggs are in the dairy category because they are a protein that needs hydrochloric acid (HCl) to digest, as do other dairy products. Buy eggs, preferably in paper cartons, laid by free-range happy chickens—organic or from your local farmer. Nothing tastes as good as a fresh farm egg. Eggs are the easiest proteins to digest. **Kefir,** a cultured, enzyme-rich food filled with friendly microorganisms, supplies complete protein, essential minerals and valuable B vitamins. It may be substituted equally in recipes for whole milk. **Sour cream,** another cultured or fermented dairy product, is generally made with milk fat, which, like butter, seems to digest easily. The souring process breaks down the milk molecule, further aiding digestion. A little maple syrup whipped into some sour cream makes a great **whipped cream**. Reported to be the number one food responsible for allergies, pasteurized milk takes an enormous amount of energy and enzymes to break down. **Yogurt** is a "predigested" dairy product because the milk molecule is thoroughly broken down. It is a great replacement for milk in baking because it is one of the easiest-to-digest foods. Yogurt diluted with water to the consistency of milk is substituted for milk in most recipes here. To prevent the yogurt taste from overpowering a recipe, **Yogurt Cheese** may be used in recipes. Yogurt Cheese is yogurt that has most of its liquid, or whey, drained. Yogurt Cheese can be substituted for cream cheese or sour cream in recipes and diluted to the consistency of milk as a mild-tasting alternative.

yogurt cheese

Makes 2 cups.

32 ounces **yogurt** (2 pounds)

Put yogurt into a yogurt strainer. A regular strainer lined with cheesecloth or a cheesecloth bag suspended over a bowl will also work. Cover and leave in the refrigerator for at least 3 hours. Yogurt Cheese becomes thicker the longer it is allowed to drain. Its thickest point should be reached in 24 hours. Pour off the whey and store the cheese in an airtight container in the refrigerator for up to 9 days.

NOTE: A mesh yogurt strainer may be used to drain and store the yogurt cheese. For a yogurt strainer by Donvier, see "Sources."

seeds and nuts

The Aztecs soaked **seeds** in brine (salted water), then laid them in the sun to dry. Salt neutralizes enzyme inhibitors, making seeds and nuts easier to digest. **Nuts** are a great source of proteins, oils and nutrients, but they can be very difficult to digest unless they are soaked or sprouted. Like unsprouted grains, nuts contain enzyme inhibitors that make them hard to digest. Unsprouted nuts and seeds need large amounts of hydrochloric acid and bile (the soap-like substance from the liver and gallbladder that breaks down fats) to break them down. Soaking nuts and sprouting seeds makes their nutrients more accessible to the body, and these are wonderful additions to baked goods. The following recipe has been included for those who wish to incorporate prepared nuts into their diet.

preparing nuts

This simple process involves soaking nuts in saltwater and then drying them slowly. It is important to start with fresh, whole, organic raw nuts. Both nuts with skin and skinless nuts may be soaked. Hazelnuts, almonds, cashews and pecans are a few of my favorites.

The proportion for soaking and drying nuts is as follows:

1 cup **raw nuts** such as **hazelnuts, almonds, pecans, walnuts and cashews**
1 ½ teaspoons **sea salt**
Water

Place the nuts and sea salt in a bowl and cover with room-temperature water. Let them soak for 8 hours (*no* longer than 6 hours for cashews).

Preheat the oven to 150°F. Drain the nuts and spread them in a single layer on a stainless steel baking pan. Dry the nuts in the warm oven for 12 to 24 hours, stirring occasionally, until they are very dry and crisp. A dehydrator may be used instead of an oven.

Once the nuts have been soaked and dried, they may be stored in an airtight container and refrigerated or frozen for many months.

miscellaneous

Chocolate is not used in these recipes because it is a hard-to-digest food item, which contains caffeine. After being picked, fermented and dried, cacao beans go through a gentle heating and grinding process, leaving 70 percent cocoa butter and 30 percent chocolate solids. Ingredients are then added to chocolate, making it even harder to digest than it already is. Once the chocolate is smooth, it is poured to form the unsweetened chocolate squares used for baking. Raw chocolate, or **cacao**, is the absolute best form of chocolate because there is no added sugar and it has never been through a heating process, and this makes it easier to digest. Cacao is available at health food stores in powder and nib form (a grated chip), which you can add to recipes as desired. It does, however, contain caffeine, which is difficult for most bodies to process. **Water** is a major ingredient in baking. It is important to use safe, clean, fresh water. As with other ingredients, always try to use the best-quality water available. Some municipal water or tap water contains high levels of chlorine. Hard water can contain heavy minerals. If you are experiencing less-than-satisfactory results from your baking, consider using filtered water.

A Note about Equipment

With this list of basic equipment, you will be able to bake any recipe in this book. Of course, you can always add to your repertoire as needed or when you want to experiment with different techniques. If you are just beginning to bake, start simple. With a bowl and a wooden spoon you can whip up muffins, pancake batter, pizza dough or bread. Gather the equipment you need as you go along. Baking is personal, and everyone has their own personal touch.

Always use safe cookware and bakeware. The only materials we recommend for cookware and bakeware are stainless steel, cast iron, enameled cast iron, ceramic or pottery, silicone and glass as approved for cooking. Do not use any other material, especially the nonstick variety, except stainless steel nonstick bakeware that uses titanium oxide as the coating, which is nontoxic.

Pampered Chef® offers a line of stoneware that is great for baking. The Bundt pan is especially wonderful. All Clad® offers a line of stainless steel bakeware including jellyroll, square and rectangular pans. They are a bit pricy but come with a lifetime warranty and are amazing baking pans. Treat yourself. If you have aluminum baking pans, consider covering them with Silpat® nonstick liners, which are made from silicone and are nontoxic. (See "Sources.") Also, paper muffin cup liners can be used in aluminum muffin tins.

basic baking equipment

Buying quality equipment ensures better baking results and saves on replacement costs in the long run. Of course, support your local cooking supply shops first, but many items are available online with free shipping. (See "Sources.")

— Blender
— Cheesecloth or Donvier® Wave Yogurt Strainer
— Colander
— Cookie pan/jellyroll, stainless steel
— Food processor
— Grater
— Knife, sharp (we like Henckel® or Wüsthof®)

- Measuring cups and spoons, glass and/or stainless steel
- Mixer, standing and/or hand
- Mixing bowls, glass, pottery or stainless steel
- Muffin tins, stainless steel (aluminum pans can be lined with paper cups or use Silpat® nonstick liners)
- Pizza/baking stone or cast-iron pizza pan
- Pizza peel (a wooden paddle for sliding pizza in and out of the oven)
- Pots and pans, stainless steel, glass, stoneware, ceramic or silicone
  - Bundt pan
  - Cookie sheet/jellyroll
  - Loaf pan
  - Pie pan
  - Rectangular pan, 9- by 13-inch
  - Round pan, 8- or 9-inch
  - Springform pan, 9- or 10-inch
  - Square pan, 8-inch
  - Stockpot
- Spatula, stainless steel, wood or silicone
- Waffle maker
- Whisk, stainless steel, wood or silicone

Recipes

These recipes have been developed and successfully tested using Essential Eating Sprouted Foods certified organic sprouted whole grain wheat or sprouted spelt flour. "The Sprouted Baking Adventure" section in Chapter 3 offers information about the different personalities of the sprouted flours. Flours not certified by Essential Eating may be substituted in recipes using flour, but keep in mind that they may perform differently.

The photographs of the recipes in this book are authentic. The food has not been glued, sprayed, colored or, as is sometimes the case, substituted, such as paste being used as icing. We wanted the photos in this book to be authentic and the recipes to be photographed as they were prepared in the Essential Eating demo kitchen to look like real food should look. Because nothing else has been added, the dishes look the same as they will when you make them.

Bread, Rolls and Crackers

Sandwich Bread and Rolls

Makes one 2-pound loaf or 12 rolls.

4	tablespoons room-temperature **butter**
4	tablespoons **maple syrup**
1½	cups room-temperature **water**
4	cups **Essential Eating Sprouted Flour**
1½	teaspoons **sea salt**
2	teaspoons **yeast**

FOR SANDWICH BREAD: Place the room-temperature wet ingredients in a bread maker and add the dry ingredients on top, ending with the yeast. Set the program for the basic rapid cycle and press start.

If you prefer to mix by hand, place the dry ingredients in a large bowl; add the wet ingredients. Mix until the dough forms. Remove the dough from the bowl and knead about 8 minutes until it is smooth and elastic. Grease the bowl with olive oil and place the dough in the bowl. Cover it with a dry dish towel and let it rise in a warm place until double, about 1 hour. Punch down the dough, form it into a loaf and place it in a greased loaf pan. Let it rise until double. Preheat the oven to 350°F. Bake 15–18 minutes. Remove it from the pan and cool on a wire rack.

FOR ROLLS: Set the program for the dough setting on the machine or mix by hand as above. Let the dough rise until double; punch it down. Cut the dough into 12 pieces and form them into 12 rolls; place them on a greased baking sheet 2 inches apart. Let the rolls rise until double again. Preheat the oven to 350°F. Bake 12–15 minutes, until golden brown.

NOTE: For variation, poppy seeds; herbs; chopped, moist sun-dried tomatoes; or olives may be added to the bread and rolls.

Sweet Potato Rolls

In a large bowl, dissolve the yeast in the warm water and let it stand 5 minutes. Fold in the yogurt. Whisk in the sweet potato puree, 1 tablespoon butter, salt and egg yolks. Lightly spoon the flour into a dry measuring cup; level with a knife. Add 3½ cups of the flour; stir until a soft dough forms.

2¼	teaspoons	**yeast**
½	cup lukewarm	**water**
½	cup	**yogurt**
¾	cup canned	**sweet potato puree**
1	tablespoon	**butter**, melted
1¼	teaspoons	**sea salt**
2	large	**egg yolks**, lightly beaten
4	cups	**Essential Eating Sprouted Flour**
2	tablespoons	**butter**, melted, or olive oil

Turn the dough out onto a floured surface. Knead it until it is smooth and elastic (about 8 minutes); add enough of the remaining flour, 1 tablespoon at a time, to prevent the dough from sticking to your hands (it will feel soft and tacky). Place the dough in a large bowl coated with olive oil, turning to coat the top. Cover and let it rise in a warm place, 45 minutes or until doubled in size. Punch down the dough, cover it and let it rest 5 minutes.

Line two baking sheets with parchment paper. Divide the dough into 24 equal pieces. Cover half to prevent drying. Shape each piece into a 9-inch rope and tie it into a knot, tucking the ends under the roll and placing it on the prepared sheet. Repeat with the remaining dough pieces. Cover each sheet with a dry dish towel and let the rolls rise 30–45 minutes, or until doubled in size.

Preheat the oven to 400°F. Uncover the rolls. Place both baking sheets in the oven and bake for 8 minutes. Rotate the pans from top to bottom; bake an additional 6–8 minutes, or until the rolls are golden brown on top and sound hollow when tapped on the bottom. Remove them from the pans and cool on wire racks. Brush the rolls with 2 tablespoons melted butter or olive oil.

Herbed Baguettes

1½	cups room-temperature **water**
¼	cup **maple syrup**
4	teaspoons room-temperature **butter**
4½	cups **Essential Eating Sprouted Flour**
1½	teaspoons **sea salt**
¼	teaspoon **lemon pepper**
4	tablespoons dried **dill**, or 6 tablespoons fresh dill
2¼	teaspoons **yeast**

To make the dough with a bread machine, place the ingredients, in the order listed, in the pan of the bread machine. Set the program for the dough setting and press start. When the dough cycle is complete, remove it from the pan; shape it into two or three baguettes. Place the baguettes on a greased baking sheet and cover with a dry dish towel. Let them rise in a warm place about 45 minutes to 1 hour, or until double. Preheat the oven to 350°F. Bake 18–20 minutes, until light brown.

To mix by hand, place the dry ingredients in a large bowl and add the wet ingredients. Mix until the dough forms. Remove the dough from the bowl and knead it about 8 minutes, until it is soft and smooth. Grease the bowl with olive oil and place the dough in the bowl. Cover it with a dry dish towel and let it rise in a warm place until double, about 1 hour. Punch down the dough and form it into baguettes. Place the baguettes on a greased baking sheet. Preheat the oven to 350°F. Bake 30–40 minutes, until golden brown. Bread may also be baked on a baking stone.

Quinoa Whole Grain Bread

Makes one 1½-pound loaf.

1	cup room-temperature **water**
2½	teaspoons room-temperature **butter**
4	tablespoons **maple syrup**
1	teaspoon **sea salt**
3	cups **Essential Eating Sprouted Flour**
¼	cup uncooked **quinoa**
1½	teaspoons **yeast**

Place the ingredients, in the order listed, in the pan of a bread machine. Program the bread machine for a 1½-pound basic loaf and press start. For a 2-pound loaf, increase the ingredients by half. Refer to the Sandwich Bread recipe on page 44 to make this recipe by hand.

Crusty Artisan Bread

Cold fermentation creates an amazingly delicious bread. This recipe has been adapted from Artisan Bread in Five Minutes a Day, by Jeff Hertzberg and Zoë Francois (Thomas Dunne Books, 2007). A variety of wonderful artisan bread recipes are featured in their book.

Makes four 1-pound loaves.

3¼ cups lukewarm **water**
2½ tablespoons **yeast**
2   teaspoons **sea salt**
6½ cups **Essential Eating Sprouted Flour**
    Cornmeal for dusting

EQUIPMENT: Pizza peel
            Baking stone

In a large bowl, mix the water, yeast and salt. Mix in the flour using a spoon. Place a plate on top to cover the bowl and allow the dough to rest at room temperature for 2 hours, until the dough rises and collapses. The dough may be divided and baked into loaves immediately or refrigerated, covered (plate on top of bowl) but not airtight, for use over the next 14 days.

To bake, simply dust the surface of the refrigerated dough with flour. With a sharp knife, cut off a 1-pound piece, about the size of a grapefruit (4 loaves total). Dust the piece with more flour and quickly shape it into a ball by stretching the surface of the dough around to the bottom. Place the dough on a cornmeal-dusted pizza peel to rest and set a timer for 20 minutes. A large wooden cutting board or a rimless baking sheet covered with parchment paper may be used in place of a pizza peel, but be careful not to burn your hands when sliding the loaf onto the stone in the oven.

After 20 minutes, place the baking stone on the middle rack of the oven, along with an empty broiler tray on a lower shelf. Preheat the oven to 450°F and set the timer for an additional 20 minutes.

Now the loaf has rested and risen for 40 minutes and the oven is ready. Sprinkle the loaf liberally with flour and slash the top with a serrated knife in the form of a cross, parallel lines or a tic-tac-toe pattern. Some of the flour may be tapped off before baking. Put the cup of hot tap water within reach of the oven. Use no more than 1 cup of water to create steam. Slide the loaf onto the hot baking stone and pour water into the broiler tray; quickly close the oven door. Bake 25–30 minutes, or until the loaf is browned and hollow sounding when tapped on the bottom. Cool on a wire rack.

Hand-Rolled Pretzels

Making pretzels with sprouted flour is infinitely easier than you might think...and so worth it! Traditional pretzel flour is considered the bottom of the barrel in the milling industry, so using sprouted flour makes these a delicious and nutritious snack.

Makes 24 pretzels.

Put the lukewarm water in a large bowl. Sprinkle the yeast on top and stir until dissolved. Add the sugar, salt, oil and 3 cups of the flour; beat until smooth. Gradually add more flour to make a soft dough ball. Knead the dough by hand about 10 minutes, until smooth and elastic. Cover the bowl with a lint-free dish towel and let it rise about 1 hour, or until double. Divide the dough into 24 pieces; cover and let it rest 5 minutes. Grease 2 baking pans with ghee.

1½	cups lukewarm **water**
4½	teaspoons **yeast**
½	cup **maple sugar**
1½	teaspoons **sea salt**
⅓	cup **olive oil**
4–5	cups **Essential Eating Sprouted Flour**
1	large **egg white**
1	tablespoon **water**
	Coarse sea salt, poppy seeds or **cinnamon sugar** (optional)

Preheat the oven to 350°F. To shape the pretzels, roll each piece into a uniform 18-inch rope. Holding each end, lay the middle of the rope on the greased pan, making a semi-circle. While still holding the rope, overlap the two ends, twisting them once and then pressing them into the bottom curve of the circle. The dough may also be shaped into twenty-four 8-inch breadsticks.

Beat the egg white and water together; brush this on the pretzels. Sprinkle the pretzels with topping, if desired. Bake in a 350°F oven for 15 minutes. Reduce the oven temperature to 325°F and bake an additional 30 minutes, or until the pretzels are semihard and golden brown. Remove them from the baking sheets; cool on a wire rack.

Lemon Pepper Crackers

1¾ cups **Essential Eating Sprouted Flour**
1 tablespoon **Herbamare**
1 tablespoon **lemon pepper**
½ cup **butter**
1 tablespoon **paprika**

Preheat the oven to 425°F. In a medium bowl, combine the flour, Herbamare and lemon pepper. Cut in the butter with a pastry cutter or two knives until the mixture resembles coarse crumbs. Add 7–8 tablespoons water, or more as needed, until the dough sticks together when pressed. Divide the dough into 2 pieces and place each between 2 sheets of waxed paper. Roll each piece of dough out as thin as possible, about ⅛ inch thick. Remove the top layer of wax paper and flip the dough onto a baking sheet. Cut it into 2- by 2-inch squares and pierce them with the tines of a fork. Lightly sprinkle paprika on top. Bake 8–10 minutes, or until lightly browned. Cool on a wire rack.

Cinnamon Animal Crackers

Makes 3–4 dozen crackers.

In a medium bowl, combine the flours, arrowroot, salt, cinnamon and baking powder. In a large bowl, mix the butter, syrup, sugar and vanilla. Add the dry ingredients to the butter mixture alternately with the water, using just enough moisture to form the batter into a dough ball. Divide the dough in half, wrap it in waxed paper and refrigerate for 1 hour. Preheat the oven to 350°F. Grease 2 cookie sheets. On a lightly floured surface or between 2 sheets of waxed paper, roll out the dough to 1/8 inch thick. Remove the top layer of waxed paper and cut out animal shapes; place them 1 inch apart on a greased cookie sheet. Mix the cinnamon and sugar and sprinkle on top. Bake 12–15 minutes, until light brown. Remove the animal crackers from the oven and cool on a wire rack.

2	cups	**Essential Eating Sprouted Flour**
1	cup	**quinoa flour**
1	teaspoon	**arrowroot**
1/2	teaspoon	**sea salt**
1	teaspoon	**cinnamon**
2 1/2	teaspoons	**baking powder**
3/4	cup	room-temperature **butter**
1/4	cup	**maple syrup**
1	cup	**maple sugar**
1	teaspoon	**vanilla**
1/8–1/4	cup	**water**

TOPPING:

1	teaspoon	**cinnamon**
4	tablespoons	**maple sugar**

EQUIPMENT: Animal cookie cutters

Bagels

2	teaspoons **yeast**
¼	cup lukewarm **water**
2	tablespoons **barley malt syrup**
1	cup **water**
5	cups **Essential Eating Sprouted Flour**
2¼	teaspoons **sea salt**
1¼	cups **water**
⅓	cup **barley malt syrup**
1	gallon boiling **water**

Dissolve the yeast in the lukewarm water. Dissolve the 2 tablespoons barley malt syrup in 1 cup water. In the large bowl of a stand mixer or a food processor with a dough attachment, combine the flour and salt. Add the yeast mixture and the malt mixture and enough of the additional 1¼ cups water to form a slightly stiff dough; mix or pulse to combine until the dough is smooth and elastic, up to 4 minutes. Cover the dough with a kitchen towel and let it rise until double. (If using a food processor, remove the dough from the bowl and place it in a greased bowl to rise.)

Preheat the oven to 425°F. In a large stockpot, dissolve ⅓ cup barley malt syrup in a gallon of water and heat to a boil. Heavily grease a large cookie sheet or line it with parchment paper. Once the dough has doubled, gently divide it into 3 equal-sized balls and allow them to rest for 5 minutes. After they have rested, gently flatten each ball with the palm of your hand; cut each ball into 4 pieces, for a total of 12. Gently shape each piece into a ball by rolling it between your cupped hands. Let the balls rest on a lightly floured counter for an additional 5 minutes. Poke your thumb through the center of each ball and twirl your thumb on the counter for a few rotations to create a hole. Allow the bagels to rest a final 5 minutes.

Place three bagels at a time in the boiling water. After 30 seconds, flip each bagel with a slotted spoon. After 30 seconds more, remove the bagels one by one and place them,

2 inches apart, on a prepared baking sheet. Repeat the boiling process until all the bagels are on the sheet. Bake immediately for 20–30 minutes, or until golden brown.

NOTE: Because of the sugars in the barley malt, be sure to grease the pan heavily or line it with parchment paper, or the bagels will stick to it. Use a metal spatula to remove them promptly after baking and let them cool on a wire rack. The boiled bagels can be dipped in coarse sea salt, poppy seeds or dried onion flakes before baking.

Muffins and Biscuits

Date Muffins

Makes 12 muffins.

1 ½ cups **Essential Eating Sprouted Flour**
½ cup **maple syrup** or agave nectar
2 teaspoons **baking powder**
1 teaspoon **cinnamon**
¼ teaspoon **sea salt**
¼ teaspoon **nutmeg**
2 large **eggs**
⅔ cup **yogurt**
½ cup **butter**, melted
½ cup chopped **dates**
½ cup chopped prepared **almonds** (optional; see "Ingredients Matter")

In a bowl, combine the flour, maple syrup or agave nectar, baking powder, cinnamon, salt and nutmeg. In another bowl, whisk together the eggs, yogurt and butter. Stir this mixture into the dry ingredients, and whip or beat with a hand mixer briefly until well mixed. Fold in the dates and almonds.

Fill greased or paper-lined cups of a muffin tin two-thirds full. Bake at 400°F for 15–20 minutes, or until a toothpick comes out clean. Cool for 5 minutes before removing to a wire rack.

Cranberry Citrus Muffins

Makes 12 muffins.

Preheat the oven to 375°F. In a small bowl, combine the cranberries and the 2 tablespoons of flour; toss gently and set aside. Measure the remaining 2 cups of flour into a large bowl by gently spooning it into a measuring cup and leveling it off with a knife. Add the 1 cup of sugar, the baking powder and the salt. Whisk together the butter and the next 5 ingredients in a medium bowl. Make a well in the center of the flour mixture; add the butter mixture, stirring just until the flour mixture is moist. Fold in the cranberry mixture. Spoon the batter into a muffin tin lined with paper cups or greased with ghee. Sprinkle the remaining 2 teaspoons of sugar on the muffins before baking. Bake 25–30 minutes. Remove the muffins from the tin and place on a wire rack to cool.

1 ½ cups chopped fresh or frozen **cranberries**
2 tablespoons **Essential Eating Sprouted Flour**
2 cups **Essential Eating Sprouted Flour**
1 cup **maple sugar**
2 teaspoons **baking powder**
½ teaspoon **sea salt**
½ cup room-temperature **butter**
1 teaspoon grated **lemon rind**
½ teaspoon **vanilla**
2 large **egg whites**
1 cup **yogurt**
1 large **egg**
2 teaspoons **maple sugar**

Sweet Rolls

1½ cups lukewarm **water**
2¼ teaspoons **yeast**
  4 tablespoons room-temperature **butter**
⅓ cup **maple syrup**
4½ cups **Essential Eating Sprouted Flour**
1½ teaspoons **sea salt**

FILLING:
¼ cup **maple sugar**
1½ teaspoons **cinnamon**
⅓ cup **raisins** (optional)

GLAZE:
½ cup **maple syrup**

TO PREPARE THE DOUGH: Put the lukewarm water in a large bowl and dissolve the yeast; let it stand 5 minutes until foamy. Add the butter and syrup to the yeast mixture and mix well. Add 4 cups of the flour and the salt, stirring until a soft dough forms. Turn the dough out onto a floured surface. Knead it until it is smooth and elastic, about 8 minutes; add enough of the remaining flour, 1 tablespoon at a time, to prevent the dough from sticking to your hands (it will feel slightly sticky). Place the dough in a large bowl coated with mild olive oil or ghee. Cover and let it rise in a warm place for 1 hour, or until double. Gently press two fingers into the dough. If the indentation remains, the dough has risen enough. Punch down the dough; roll it into a 16- by 12-inch rectangle on a floured surface.

FOR THE FILLING: In a small bowl, mix the sugar and cinnamon. Leaving a ½-inch border around the edges, sprinkle this mixture over the dough. If using raisins, sprinkle them over the surface and press them gently into the dough.

Roll up the rectangle tightly, starting with a long edge, and press it firmly to eliminate air pockets; pinch the seam to seal it. Cut the dough into 9 rolls. Place the rolls, cut sides up, in a 9-inch round baking pan coated with ghee or butter. Cover and let them rise 45 minutes, or until doubled in size.

Preheat the oven to 375°F. Uncover the rolls, pour the remaining $1/2$ cup of syrup on top and bake for 22 minutes, or until lightly browned. Cool in the pan on a wire rack.

Carrot Cake Muffins

Makes 12 muffins.

Preheat the oven to 350°F. In a large bowl, cream the butter and syrup. Beat in the yogurt, eggs and vanilla. Combine the flour, cinnamon, baking powder and salt. Add the dry ingredients to the creamed mixture and mix well. Stir in the grated carrots. Grease or line 12 cups of a standard muffin tin. Spoon the batter into the cups and bake 18–20 minutes, until a toothpick inserted in the center comes out clean. Cool in the muffin tin for 5 minutes; remove to a wire rack to continue cooling.

¼ cup room-temperature **butter**
1 cup **maple syrup**
¼ cup **yogurt**
3 large **eggs**
½ teaspoon **vanilla**
1 ¼ cups **Essential Eating Sprouted Flour**
1 teaspoon **cinnamon**
1 ½ teaspoons **baking powder**
¼ teaspoon **sea salt**
1 cup grated **carrots**

Cream Cheese Frosting

Makes about 1½ cups.

1 8-ounce package **cream cheese**
5 tablespoons **butter**
⅓ cup **maple sugar**
1 teaspoon **vanilla**

Using an electric mixer, beat the cream cheese and butter together until smooth and creamy. Add the vanilla, and blend. Add the sugar slowly to blend. Mix on high until the sugar has dissolved and the frosting is velvety smooth.

Sweet Cornbread

½   cup **corn flour**
1   cup **cornmeal**
½   cup **Essential Eating Sprouted Flour**
1½ teaspoons **baking powder**
1   teaspoon **sea salt**
2   large **egg whites**
¼   cup **yogurt**
½   cup **water**
¼   cup **butter**, melted
½   cup **maple syrup**
1   cup frozen **corn kernels**, thawed

Preheat the oven to 375°F. In a large bowl, mix the dry ingredients. In a separate bowl, beat together the egg whites, yogurt, water, butter and syrup. Add the flour mixture to the liquids. Blend the ingredients and fold in the corn kernels. Pour the batter into a greased 8-inch square baking pan. Bake 25–30 minutes, or until done.

Coconut Scones

Preheat the oven to 425°F. Stack 2 baking sheets on top of each other to prevent the biscuit bottoms from overbrowning while baking; line the top pan with parchment paper. In a large bowl, mix the flour, sugar, baking powder, baking soda, coconut and salt. Cut in the butter with a pastry blender until it forms a coarse crumb mixture. Add the yogurt to the flour mixture and mix until the flour is incorporated and the dough sticks together. In a small bowl, combine the egg and water to make the egg wash.

2 ¼	cups	**Essential Eating Sprouted Flour**
¼	cup	**maple sugar**
3	tablespoons	**baking powder**
½	teaspoon	**baking soda**
¼	cup dried,	**shredded coconut**
¼	teaspoon	**sea salt**
½	cup	**butter**
⅔	cup	**yogurt**

EGG WASH:

1	large	**egg**
1	tablespoon	**water**

On a well-floured surface, knead the dough gently 4 or 5 times and pat it into a 7-inch circle about 1 inch thick. Cut the circle in half and cut each half into 3 equal pie-shaped wedges; transfer to the prepared pan. Brush the tops with the egg wash, and bake 15–20 minutes, or until golden brown.

Herbed Sweet Potato Biscuits

1 pound **sweet potatoes** or yams, scrubbed, or one 15-ounce can sweet potato puree

2 cups **Essential Eating Sprouted Flour**

1 teaspoon dried ground **sage**, rosemary or thyme

2 tablespoons **maple sugar**

4 teaspoons **baking powder**

½ teaspoon **sea salt**

6 tablespoons **butter**

¼ cup **yogurt**

¼ cup **water**

1 large **egg yolk** mixed with 1 tablespoon **water**

30 small sprigs of **sage**, rosemary or thyme (optional)

Preheat the oven to 425°F. If using whole sweet potatoes, pierce them all over with a fork, set on a cookie sheet and bake for 1 hour, or until tender. Let them cool slightly. Spoon the potato flesh from the skins into a bowl and mash with a fork; you should have 1½ cups of mashed sweet potatoes. Refrigerate until chilled.

In a large bowl, mix the flour with the dried herb, sugar, baking powder and salt. Cut in the butter with a pastry blender until it forms a coarse crumb mixture. Remove the sweet potatoes from the refrigerator and mix in the yogurt and water. Add the potato mixture to the flour mixture and stir until the flour is incorporated and the dough sticks together. Refrigerate the dough for at least 15 minutes.

Preheat the oven to 425°F. Stack 2 baking sheets on top of each other to prevent the biscuit bottoms from overbrowning while baking; line the top pan with parchment paper. On a well-floured surface, pat out the dough until it is 1 inch thick. Using a floured 2-inch round cutter, stamp out as many biscuits as possible, being careful not to twist the cutter; transfer them to the prepared pan. Roll the scraps together and stamp out more biscuits. Brush the tops of the biscuits with the egg wash and press a small herb sprig into each one. Bake 18–20 minutes, or until golden brown. Serve warm or at room temperature.

Zucchini Power Muffins

Makes 12 muffins.

Preheat the oven to 375°F. Grease and flour a muffin tin, or use paper liners. In a large bowl, combine the flours and sugar. Stir in the baking powder, baking soda, cinnamon, nutmeg and salt. Cut in the butter until the mixture resembles coarse crumbs. Make a well in the center, and pour in the yogurt, eggs, zucchini and vanilla. Fold in the raisins.

Fill muffin cups ³/₄ full. Sprinkle the tops with the maple sugar. Bake 18–20 minutes, or until a toothpick inserted into the center comes out clean. Remove and cool on a wire rack.

1¾	cups **Essential Eating Sprouted Flour**
¼	cup **quinoa flour**
1	cup **date sugar** or maple sugar
2½	teaspoons **baking powder**
½	teaspoon **baking soda**
1	teaspoon **cinnamon**
1	teaspoon **nutmeg**
½	teaspoon **sea salt**
½	cup **butter**
¼	cup **yogurt**
2	large **eggs**, lightly beaten
1½	cups shredded **zucchini**
1	teaspoon **vanilla**
½	cup raisins or **dates**
¼	cup **maple sugar** for topping
¼	cup **water**

Maple Banana Muffins

6	tablespoons **butter**, melted
½	cup **maple syrup**
2	large **eggs**, lightly beaten
4	ripe **bananas**, mashed
1¼	cups **Essential Eating Sprouted Flour**
1	cup **cornmeal**
2	teaspoons **baking powder**
½	teaspoon **baking soda**
½	teaspoon **sea salt**

Preheat the oven to 375°F. Grease or line 12 cups of a standard muffin tin. In a large bowl, blend the butter and syrup. Add the eggs and bananas. Mix in the remaining ingredients. Pour the batter into the prepared muffin tin. Bake 16–18 minutes, until the muffin tops are golden and a tester inserted into the center of the muffins comes out clean. Transfer to a rack and cool.

Pumpkin Cornmeal Muffins

Makes 12 muffins.

Preheat the oven to 375°F. Grease or line 12 cups of a standard muffin tin. In a large bowl, combine the flour, cornmeal, baking powder, cinnamon, baking soda and salt. In a medium bowl, beat together the butter, egg, syrup, molasses, sour cream and pumpkin. Mix the wet ingredients into the dry ingredients until combined. The batter will have a lumpy consistency. Spoon the batter into the prepared pan, filling the cups almost to the top. Bake until golden brown and a cake tester inserted into the center comes out clean, about 20 minutes.

1	cup **Essential Eating Sprouted Flour**
1	cup **cornmeal**
2	teaspoons **baking powder**
1	teaspoon **cinnamon**
½	teaspoon **baking soda**
½	teaspoon **sea salt**
¼	cup **butter**, melted
1	large **egg**
¾	cup **maple syrup**
2	tablespoons **molasses**
¾	cup **sour cream**
½	cup canned **pumpkin puree**

Let stand 10 minutes on a wire rack before turning the muffins out of the cups to cool. Serve them hot, warm or at room temperature.

NOTE: Maple syrup may be substituted for molasses.

Strawberry Shortcake

Makes 8 servings.

1¾ cups **Essential Eating Sprouted Flour**
¼ cup **maple sugar**
1½ tablespoons **baking powder**
⅛ teaspoon **salt**
⅓ cup **butter**
1 large **egg**
1 teaspoon **vanilla**
½ cup **yogurt**

EGG WASH:
1 large **egg**
1 tablespoon **water**

FILLING:
2 pounds fresh **strawberries,** hulled and sliced
¼ cup **maple sugar**

TOPPING:
¼ cup **maple syrup**
1 cup **sour cream**

Preheat the oven to 425°F. Stack 2 baking sheets on top of each other to prevent the biscuit bottoms from overbrowning while baking; line the top pan with parchment paper. In a large bowl, mix the flour, sugar, baking powder and salt. Cut in the butter with a pastry blender until it forms a coarse crumb mixture. Combine the egg, vanilla and yogurt; add this to the flour mixture and mix until the flour is incorporated and the dough sticks together.

On a well-floured surface, knead the dough gently 4 or 5 times and pat it into a circle about 1 inch thick. Cut the circle in half and cut each half into 3 equal pie-shaped wedges; transfer to the prepared pan. In a small bowl, combine the egg and water to make the egg wash. Brush the tops with the egg wash, and bake 15–20 minutes, or until golden brown.

In a medium bowl combine the strawberries and sugar; let them marinate while the cakes bake and cool. For the topping, in a large bowl whip the syrup and sour cream with a whisk until creamy. Cut or break the biscuits in half, place the bottom half on a plate and top with some of the strawberry mixture. Place the top half on the strawberries and top with the whipped cream. Drizzle juice from the strawberries over the top.

Cakes, Pies and Tarts

Banana Cake

2¼ cups **Essential Eating Sprouted Flour**
½ teaspoon **baking powder**
1 teaspoon **baking soda**
½ teaspoon **sea salt**
1 teaspoon **cinnamon**
1 teaspoon **nutmeg**
½ cup **butter**
1½ cups **maple sugar**
2 large **eggs**
1 cup lightly mashed **bananas**, about 2 medium
1 teaspoon **vanilla**
¼ cup **yogurt** or sour cream
Maple cream for topping

Preheat the oven to 350°F. In a medium bowl, combine the first 6 dry ingredients; mix. In the bowl of an electric mixer, cream the butter until it is fluffy, then add the sugar and beat again until fluffy. Add the eggs, one at a time, mixing between additions. In a third bowl, mash the bananas with the vanilla and yogurt. Add the flour mixture to the butter mixture in two parts, alternating with the banana mixture. After each addition, stir the batter until smooth. Pour into a greased silicone or stoneware Bundt pan and bake for 25–30 minutes. Allow the silicone pan to cool completely before inverting it onto a serving platter. Let the stoneware pan cool 20 minutes before inverting it onto a platter. Drizzle with maple cream before serving.

Blueberry Cornmeal Cake

Makes 9 servings.

Preheat the oven to 350°F. Toss the blueberries with 1 tablespoon of the flour and set them aside. In a large bowl, mix the remaining flour, cornmeal, baking powder, sugar and salt. In a small bowl, mix the yogurt, water, lemon juice, egg and melted butter. Add the liquids to the dry ingredients and mix just until blended. Gently fold in the blueberries. Spoon the batter into a greased 8- by 8-inch pan. Sprinkle it with the cinnamon sugar. Bake for 35–40 minutes, or until the cake is golden and a toothpick inserted into the center comes out clean. If necessary, cover it loosely with foil during the last 15 minutes to prevent excess browning.

1	cup fresh or frozen (not thawed) **blueberries**
1	tablespoon **Essential Eating Sprouted Flour**
1½	cups **Essential Eating Sprouted Flour**
½	cup **cornmeal**
2	teaspoons **baking powder**
⅔	cup **maple sugar**
½	teaspoon **sea salt**
½	cup **yogurt**
¼	cup **water**
1	tablespoon fresh **lemon juice**
1	large **egg**
½	cup **butter**, melted
2	teaspoons **cinnamon sugar** (equal mixture of each)

Cherry Tart

CRUST:

3¾ cups **Essential Eating Sprouted Flour**

⅓ cup **maple sugar**

½ teaspoon **sea salt**

1½ cups cold **butter**, cut into small cubes

3 large **egg yolks**, lightly beaten

3–6 tablespoons ice **water**

FILLING:

6 cups fresh or frozen **cherries** (two 10-ounce bags)

⅓ cup **maple sugar**

4 tablespoons **lemon juice**

2 teaspoons **arrowroot**

1 pinch **sea salt**

FOR THE CRUST: In the bowl of a food processor, pulse the flour, sugar and salt until combined, about 4 times. Add the butter and process until the mixture resembles coarse meal, about 10 seconds. With the processor running, add the egg yolks. Gradually pour in the water; process until the dough begins to come together, no more than 30 seconds. Pat the dough into a disk shape. The dough may be wrapped in waxed paper and refrigerated for later use.

Place a piece of parchment paper the size of a large baking sheet on the counter. Dust with flour and roll out an oval crust approximately ⅛ inch thick or less. To create the edges, fold over the dough to make a ½-to 1-inch border. Place the parchment paper with the crust on a baking sheet in preparation for baking.

FOR THE FILLING: Preheat the oven to 350°F. In a medium bowl, combine all the filling ingredients. Let the mixture sit for 15 minutes, stirring occasionally. Pour the cherry mixture into a small strainer over a medium saucepan, allowing the juice to flow into the saucepan. Place the strained cherries onto the prepared crust and dot with approximately 2 tablespoons cubed butter. Bake for about 25 minutes.

Meanwhile, heat the remaining cherry juice in a saucepan over medium heat, stirring occasionally, until it thickens into a light syrup. Remove from the heat and set aside.

When the tart has finished baking, remove it from the oven and place the sheet on a wire rack to cool. Before serving, pour the cherry glaze over the tart.

NOTE: Recipe makes 1 large or 3 small tarts.

Rhubarb Cake

Preheat the oven to 350°F. Grease and flour a 13- by 9- by 2-inch pan. For the crumb topping, mix ½ cup of the sugar, the melted butter and the cinnamon until crumbly, and set aside. In a separate bowl, cream together the remaining 1½ cups of sugar, the ½ cup of butter and the egg. In a small bowl, mix the flour, baking soda and salt. Add the dry ingredients to the creamed mixture, alternating with the yogurt or sour cream. Stir in the rhubarb. Pour the mixture into the pan and sprinkle with reserved crumb topping. Bake for 40–45 minutes. Cut into squares and serve warm or cool with Whipped Cream Topping.

½ cup **maple sugar**
1 tablespoon **butter**, melted
1½ cups **maple sugar**
1 teaspoon **cinnamon**
½ cup **butter**
1 large **egg**
2 cups **Essential Eating Sprouted Flour**
1 teaspoon **baking soda**
½ teaspoon **sea salt**
1 cup **yogurt** or sour cream
1½ cups chopped **rhubarb**

Whipped Cream Topping

Makes enough for 1 cake.

½ cup **maple syrup**
2 cups **sour cream**

In a large bowl, whisk together the maple syrup and sour cream until creamy.

Cakes, Pies and Tarts

Yellow Cupcakes

Makes 12 cupcakes.

1¾ cups **Essential Eating Sprouted Flour**
½   teaspoon **sea salt**
1   cup **maple sugar**
2   large **eggs**
½   cup **water**
2   tablespoons **yogurt**
½   cup room-temperature **butter**
1½ teaspoons **baking powder**
1   teaspoon **vanilla**
    Maple Cream or **Caramel Frosting**

Preheat the oven to 375°F. Grease or line 12 cups of a standard muffin tin. Place the flour, salt and sugar in a mixing bowl; add the eggs, water, yogurt and butter. Using the whip attachment to your mixer, whip for 1 minute at low speed. Scrape down the sides of the bowl and whip for another minute at a slightly higher speed. Scrape the bowl and fold in the baking powder and vanilla with a spatula. Whip for 30 seconds on low speed. Pour the batter into the prepared cups. Bake 18 minutes. Cool on a wire rack. Cupcakes can be topped with Maple Cream or Caramel Frosting.

Caramel Frosting

Makes enough for 1 batch of cupcakes.

In the bowl of a stand mixer, cream the sugar and butter. To prevent the sugar dust from flying out of the bowl, drape a dish towel over the mixer and start the mixer on low. Add the salt, vanilla and 3 tablespoons of water; beat

2   cups **maple sugar**
¼   cup room-temperature **butter**
¼   teaspoon **sea salt**
1   teaspoon **vanilla**
3–4 tablespoons **water**

@

until smooth. Add the additional tablespoon of water if the frosting needs to be thinner. To thicken the frosting, add more sugar.

~~ **FOR LEMON FROSTING:** Substitute 2 tablespoons fresh-squeezed lemon juice for the water.

Coconut Cake

Makes one 2-layer cake.

Preheat the oven to 375°F. Grease two 8-inch square or round pans. In a mixing bowl, combine the flour, salt and sugar; add the eggs, water, yogurt and butter. Using the whip attachment to your mixer, whip for 1 minute at low speed. Scrape down the sides of the bowl and whip for an additional minute at a slightly higher speed. Scrape the bowl and fold in the baking powder and vanilla with a spatula.

1¾	cups **Essential Eating Sprouted Flour**
½	teaspoon **sea salt**
1	cup **maple sugar**
2	large **eggs**
½	cup **water**
2	tablespoons **yogurt**
½	cup room-temperature **butter**
1½	teaspoons **baking powder**
1	teaspoon **vanilla**

Whip for 30 seconds on low speed. Pour the batter into the prepared pans. Bake for 20 minutes. Cool in the pan before removing. Place one cooled layer on a cake platter and spread it with half of the Coconut Icing. Place the second layer on top and spread it with the remaining icing, leaving the sides of the cake unfrosted.

Coconut Icing

Makes enough for 1 cake.

2	cups **sour cream**
1	teaspoon **vanilla**
5	cups **shredded coconut**
1	cup **maple sugar**

In a large bowl, mix the sour cream, vanilla and coconut; blend well. Add the sugar, and mix thoroughly.

Peach Cranberry Cobbler

6 cups fresh or frozen **peaches** (two 10-ounce bags)
1 cup fresh or frozen **cranberries**
¾ cup **maple sugar**
1 tablespoon **arrowroot**
¾ cup **Essential Eating Sprouted Flour**
¼ cup **quinoa flakes**
⅔ cup **maple sugar**
½ cup **butter**

If using fresh peaches, slice them ½ inch thick. Preheat the oven to 375°F. Grease a 10-inch baking pan; arrange the peaches in the bottom and top with the cranberries. Fold ¾ cup of the sugar and the arrowroot into the peaches and cranberries. In a large bowl, combine the flour, quinoa flakes and the remaining ⅔ cup of sugar. Using a pastry knife, cut in the butter until the mixture is crumbly and well combined. Sprinkle the crumb mixture evenly over the fruit. Bake 25–30 minutes, until the topping is light brown.

∽ **NOTE:** Apples or other fruit may be substituted for the peaches.

Sour Cream Carob Cake

Makes one 2-layer cake.

Preheat the oven to 350°F. Grease and flour two 9-inch round cake pans; set aside. In a small bowl, combine the flour, carob powder, baking powder, baking soda and salt. In a large bowl, using a hand mixer, cream the butter and sugar on medium speed until combined. Beat in the eggs and vanilla until combined. Beat in the carob and sour cream. Alternately add the flour mixture, yogurt and water. Beat on low after each addition just until combined. Spread the batter in the prepared pans. Bake for 25 minutes, or until the tops spring back when lightly touched. Cool on wire racks for 10 minutes. Remove from the pans and cool. Place one layer on a cake plate. Spread the top with Cream Cheese Frosting. Stack the second layer on top of the first. Dust with maple sugar. To make a checkered design on the top, cut ½-inch strips of paper and lay them over the top of the cake to make a checkerboard pattern. Sprinkle with maple sugar. Remove the strips.

1 ½ cups **Essential Eating Sprouted Flour**
⅓ cup **carob powder**
1 teaspoon **baking powder**
1 teaspoon **baking soda**
½ teaspoon **sea salt**
½ cup **butter**
1 ¼ cups **maple sugar**
2 large **eggs**
1 teaspoon **vanilla**
3 ounces **carob chips**
1 cup **sour cream**
¼ cup **yogurt**
½ cup **water**
Cream Cheese Frosting (see page 71)
Maple sugar for dusting

Skillet Pumpkin Pie

CRUST:

2½	cups	**Essential Eating Sprouted Flour**, plus extra for dusting
1	tablespoon	**maple sugar**
1	teaspoon	**sea salt**
1	pinch	**cinnamon**
1	cup cold	**butter**
5	tablespoons ice	**water**

FILLING:

½	cup	**yogurt**
1½	cups	**water**
2	large	**eggs**
¾	cup	**maple syrup**
2	15-ounce cans	**pumpkin puree** or 3½ cups cooked fresh pumpkin
1	teaspoon	**baking powder**
1	teaspoon	**sea salt**
1	tablespoon	**Essential Eating Sprouted Flour**
1	tablespoon	**cinnamon**
1	teaspoon	**vanilla**
1	dash	**ginger** and ground **cloves**

FOR THE CRUST: In a medium bowl, combine the flour, sugar, salt and cinnamon. With a pastry cutter, mix in the butter until the mixture resembles coarse crumbs. Add water a tablespoon at a time and mix until the dough forms. The dough may also be made in a food processor. Put the dry ingredients in the bowl, add the butter and pulse a few seconds until the mixture resembles coarse crumbs. Add the water a tablespoon at a time and process a few more seconds until mixed through. Do not overprocess.

Flatten the ball of dough, place it between two pieces of parchment or waxed paper dusted with flour and roll out a circle two inches larger than the skillet. Lay the crust in the greased skillet.

FOR THE FILLING: Preheat the oven to 400°F. In a large bowl, combine the yogurt and water. Add the remaining ingredients in the order listed, and mix well. Pour the

filling into the crust. Bake for 10 minutes at 400°F, then reduce the temperature to 350°F and bake an additional 45–55 minutes, or until the filling has set and the crust is golden brown.

Apple Cake

Makes 16 servings.

Grease a 9- by 13-inch pan and preheat the oven to 350°F. Using an electric mixer, combine the butter and eggs; mix until creamy. Add the sugar and vanilla, mixing again until fluffy. In a separate bowl, combine the dry ingredients. Mix the dry ingredients into the wet ingredients a few spoonfuls at a time until combined. Fold in the chopped apples. Bake for 1 hour, or until golden brown. Top with Maple Cream Cheese Frosting if desired.

¾ cup **butter**
2 large **eggs**
1 cup **maple sugar**
1 teaspoon **vanilla**
2 cups **Essential Eating Sprouted Flour**
1 teaspoon **baking soda**
1 teaspoon ground **cinnamon**
1 teaspoon **sea salt**
5 cups (about 4 medium) peeled and chopped **apples**

Maple Cream Cheese Frosting

Makes enough for 1 cake.

6 ounces **cream cheese**
3 tablespoons **butter**
1 teaspoon **maple syrup**
1 teaspoon **vanilla**
2 cups **maple sugar**

Cream together the cream cheese and butter. Add the syrup and vanilla. Mix in the sugar a little at a time. Blend until fluffy.

Vegetable Quiche

CRUST:

1	cup	**Essential Eating Sprouted Flour**
¼	teaspoon	**sea salt**
5	tablespoons cold	**butter**, cubed
4	tablespoons cold	**water**

FILLING:

4	large	**eggs**
½	cup	**sour cream**
¼	cup	**Veganaise**
½	cup fresh or drained, frozen	**spinach**, chopped
½	cup shredded	**carrot**
1	small	**onion**, finely chopped
2	teaspoons	**Herbamare**
1	teaspoon	**pepper**
		Fresh **herbs** (chives, parsley, etc.) to garnish

FOR THE CRUST: Preheat the oven to 350°F. Place the flour and salt in a food processor, and pulse until combined. Add the butter cubes and continue pulsing until the texture resembles coarse meal. Continue to pulse, and slowly drizzle in the water. The flour mixture should come together in one ball. If not, scrape out the dough and form it into one smooth ball. Refrigerate the dough for 15–20 minutes if it seems too soft to roll out. Sprinkle a bit of flour on the counter and a bit more on the surface of the dough to prevent the rolling pin from sticking. Roll out the dough to fit your pie plate, leaving an extra 1/2 inch or so around the edges. Crimp the edges and poke holes in the bottom of the crust with the tines of a fork. Bake 5–7 minutes for the crust to set. Remove it from the oven. Leave the oven at 350°F while preparing the filling.

FOR THE FILLING: Using a large whisk or an electric mixer, mix all the ingredients thoroughly for 2–3 minutes. The more air that is incorporated into the mixture, the fluffier the quiche will be. Pour the filling into the par-baked crust. Bake for approximately 20 minutes,

or until set. Remove the quiche from the oven and allow it to rest on a wire rack for at least 15–20 minutes before slicing. Sprinkle with fresh herbs before serving.

Cookies and Bars

Brownie Pie

7 tablespoons **butter**, melted
⅓ cup **maple syrup** or agave nectar
⅓ cup **maple sugar**
2 tablespoons **water**
2 tablespoons **vanilla**
2 large **eggs**
⅓ cup **Essential Eating Sprouted Flour**
⅓ cup toasted or raw **quinoa flakes**
⅓ cup **carob powder**
1 teaspoon **baking powder**
¼ teaspoon **sea salt**
Maple cream

Preheat the oven to 350°F. Grease a 9-inch pie plate with ghee. In a medium bowl, mix the butter, maple syrup or agave nectar, sugar, water and vanilla; add the eggs one at a time. In a large bowl, mix the flour, quinoa flakes, carob powder, baking powder and salt. Add the wet ingredients to the dry ingredients, beating until blended. Pour into the prepared pie pan. Bake 20–25 minutes, until a toothpick inserted into the center comes out clean. Do not overbake. Drizzle maple cream over the top or spread with Maple Frosting.

Maple Frosting

Cream the sugar and butter together in a large bowl. Add the yogurt, syrup and vanilla. Beat the frosting on high until it reaches spreading consistency. Thin with maple syrup if necessary.

1½ cups **maple sugar**
¼ cup room-temperature **butter**
2 tablespoons **yogurt**
2 tablespoons **maple syrup**
½ teaspoon **vanilla**

Lemon Cornmeal Cookies

Makes 3 dozen cookies.

Position a rack in the center of the oven and preheat to 350°F. Grease 2 baking sheets. In a medium bowl, whisk together the flour, cornmeal and salt; set aside. In the bowl of an electric mixer, beat the butter, sugar, lemon juice, lemon zest and vanilla at medium-high speed until fluffy, about 2 minutes. Beat in the egg, then the yolk, beating well after each addition and scraping down the sides of the bowl as necessary. Add the flour mixture to the wet ingredients, and on low speed, mix until blended. Shape the dough into 1-inch balls and arrange them 2 inches apart on the prepared baking sheets. Moisten your palm to prevent sticking, and flatten each ball slightly. Sprinkle the cookies with maple sugar and bake, one sheet at a time, 12–14 minutes, until lightly golden around the edges. Transfer to a wire rack and cool completely.

1 ¼	cups **Essential Eating Sprouted Flour**
¾	cup yellow **cornmeal**
¼	teaspoon **sea salt**
¾	cup room-temperature **unsalted butter**
¾	cup **maple sugar**
½	teaspoon **lemon juice**
2	teaspoons finely grated **lemon zest**
½	teaspoon **vanilla**
1	large **egg**
1	large **egg yolk**
	Maple sugar for dusting

Carob Fudge Cookies

- 5 tablespoons **butter**
- ⅓ cup **carob powder**
- 1 cup **sugar**
- ⅓ cup **yogurt**
- 1 teaspoon **vanilla**
- 1 cup **Essential Eating Sprouted Flour**
- 1 teaspoon **baking soda**
- ⅛ teaspoon **salt**

Preheat the oven to 350°F. In a medium saucepan, melt the butter. Cool slightly and stir in the carob powder, sugar, yogurt and vanilla; mix. Add the flour, baking soda and salt; mix well.

Place teaspoonfuls of batter on a greased cookie sheet 2 inches apart. Bake 8–10 minutes. Remove from the oven and let the cookies cool on the pan 2–3 minutes; remove to a wire rack to cool completely.

Sugar Cookies

Makes 2 dozen cookies.

Preheat the oven to 350°F. In the bowl of a stand mixer, cream the butter and sugar; add the vanilla and eggs, and beat continually until smooth. In a separate bowl, combine the dry ingredients and add to the wet ingredients along with 1 tablespoon water. Mix thoroughly.

Roll the dough into ⅛-inch thickness and cut with cookie cutters, or roll into 1-inch balls, place on a baking sheet and flatten. Dust with cinnamon sugar and bake for 10 minutes. Remove from the cookie sheet and cool on a wire rack.

½ cup room-temperature **butter**
¾ cup **maple sugar**
1 teaspoon **vanilla**
1 large **egg**, slightly beaten
2 cups **Essential Eating Sprouted Flour**
¼ teaspoon **sea salt**
1 teaspoon **baking powder**
1 tablespoon **water**
Cinnamon maple sugar for dusting (mix together equal portions of each)

Chip Cookies

¾ cup **butter**
1¼ cups **maple sugar**
1 large **egg**
2 teaspoons **vanilla**
2½ cups **Essential Eating Sprouted Flour**
1 teaspoon **baking powder**
½ teaspoon **baking soda**
½ teaspoon **sea salt**
¾ cup **carob chips**

Preheat the oven to 350°F. In the bowl of a stand mixer, cream the butter and sugar. Add the eggs and vanilla; mix. In a medium bowl, combine the flour, baking powder, baking soda and salt. Gradually add this mixture to the butter mixture. Fold in the chips. Drop the dough by rounded tablespoonfuls onto ungreased baking sheets, 2 inches apart. Bake 8–10 minutes, or until golden brown. Cool on baking sheets for 2 minutes; remove to a wire rack to cool completely.

Pumpkin Spice Wedges

Makes 12 servings.

Preheat the oven to 375°F. Grease a 10-inch springform pan with butter or ghee. In the bowl of an electric mixer, beat the butter until creamy. Gradually add the sugar and beat on high until creamy and smooth, about 5 minutes. Add the eggs and continue beating until light and fluffy, 3–4 minutes more. In a medium bowl, combine the flour, baking powder, baking soda, salt, cinnamon, ginger and cloves. Fold half of the dry ingredients into the butter mixture and mix until creamy. Then fold in the yogurt and pumpkin and gently combine until well blended. Fold in the remaining dry ingredients and combine until thoroughly blended. Pour the batter into the prepared pan and bake until the cake springs back when touched and pulls away from the sides of the pan, 25–30 minutes. Let the cake cool on a wire rack for 5–10 minutes before removing from the pan, then continue to cool for 1 hour. Dust with maple sugar and cut into wedges.

- ½ cup room-temperature **butter**
- 1½ cups **maple sugar**
- 2 large **eggs**, lightly beaten
- 2 cups **Essential Eating Sprouted Flour**
- 2 teaspoons **baking powder**
- ½ teaspoon **baking soda**
- ½ teaspoon **sea salt**
- 1 teaspoon **cinnamon**
- 1 teaspoon **ginger**
- ½ teaspoon **cloves**
- ½ cup **yogurt**
- 1 cup **canned pumpkin puree** or cooked fresh pumpkin
- **Maple sugar** for dusting

Cookies and Bars

Variations of Biscotti

2¼ cups **Essential Eating Sprouted Flour**
1½ teaspoons **baking powder**
¼ teaspoon **sea salt**
2 large **eggs**
1¼ cups **maple sugar**
6 tablespoons room-temperature **butter**
2 teaspoons **vanilla** or almond extract
1 teaspoon **cinnamon** (optional)

Preheat the oven to 350°F. Line a baking sheet with parchment paper. In a medium bowl, combine the flour, baking powder and salt; set aside. In a large bowl, combine the eggs and sugar either by hand or using a mixer, and beat until thickened, about 3 minutes. Add the butter and vanilla or almond extract; beat until blended. Add the dry ingredients, a little at a time, and beat until incorporated. Stir in the remaining ingredients for the variation you are making. The dough will be slightly sticky.

Scoop out half the dough onto the prepared baking sheet and form into a log 12 inches long by 3 inches wide. Repeat with the remaining dough, spacing the logs 3 inches apart. Use wet fingertips to smooth the surface of the logs if needed.

Bake the logs until crisp and golden on the outside, 20–25 minutes. Remove from the oven. Reduce the oven temperature to 300°F. Let the logs cool on the baking sheet for 10 minutes. Using a wide spatula, transfer the logs to a cutting board. Using a serrated knife, cut each log into ³/₄-inch diagonal slices. Place the slices, cut side down, at least ¹/₂ inch apart, back on the baking sheet. Return them to the oven and bake 17–22 minutes, until the cookies are crisp and brown. The interiors will become crisper as they cool. Remove from the oven and cool the cookies on a wire rack.

꩜ FOR COCONUT BISCOTTI: Add 1¹/₂ cups unsweetened, shredded coconut

꩜ FOR CRANBERRY BISCOTTI: Add 1 cup dried cranberries

꩜ FOR CAROB BISCOTTI: Add 1 cup carob chips

Lemon Squares

Preheat the oven to 350°F. In a large bowl, combine the flour, sugar and salt. With a pastry knife, cut the butter into the mixture until it resembles fine crumbs. Press the dough into an 8- by 8-inch baking pan. Bake 15 minutes, or until the crust is lightly browned.

In a large bowl, beat the eggs until blended; beat in the sugar. Add the zest and gradually fold in the lemon juice. Gradually add the flour and baking powder; blend until smooth. Pour the mixture into the prepared crust. Bake 25 minutes. Cool in the pan on a wire rack. Using a sharp knife, cut into squares and dust with sugar.

CRUST:
- 1¼ cups **Essential Eating Sprouted Flour**
- 1 tablespoon **maple sugar**
- ¼ teaspoon **sea salt**
- ½ cup **butter**

FILLING:
- 2 large **eggs**
- 1 cup **maple sugar**
- 2 teaspoons grated **lemon zest**
- ¼ cup **lemon juice**
- 2 tablespoons **Essential Eating Sprouted Flour**
- ½ teaspoon **baking powder**
- **Maple sugar** for dusting

Pizza Cookie

¾ cup **Essential Eating Sprouted Flour**
½ teaspoon **baking powder**
¼ teaspoon **baking soda**
⅛ teaspoon **sea salt**
¾ cup **quinoa flakes**
⅓ cup **butter**
⅔ cup **maple sugar**
½ teaspoon **vanilla**
1 large **egg**
1 cup **raisins**

Preheat the oven to 375°F. Set out a 12-inch pizza pan or cookie sheet. In a large bowl, combine the flour, baking powder, baking soda and salt. Stir in the quinoa flakes. In the bowl of an electric mixer, beat the butter and sugar on high speed until creamy. Add the vanilla and egg, beating until just blended. Mix in the dry ingredients including the raisins. Spread the dough on the pan, making a 12-inch round. Bake for 12–15 minutes, or until golden. Cool completely in the pan. Cut into wedges.

Coconut Crisp Cookies

Preheat the oven to 325°F. Lightly grease 1 or 2 baking sheets. In a medium bowl, combine the flour, quinoa flakes, baking soda, salt and cinnamon. In a large bowl, by hand or with an electric mixer, cream the sugar and butter until blended. Add the coconut and egg and stir until blended. Stir in the flour mixture, about 1/2 cup at a time. Spoon the dough by heaping tablespoonfuls onto the prepared baking sheet(s), spacing the cookies about 2 inches apart. Bake 12 minutes, until golden brown. Remove from the oven and let cool on the pan 5 minutes before removing to a wire rack to cool completely.

1	cup	**Essential Eating Sprouted Flour**
1	cup	**quinoa flakes**
1	teaspoon	**baking soda**
1/4	teaspoon	**salt**
1/4	teaspoon	**cinnamon**
3/4	cup	**maple sugar**
6	tablespoons	room-temperature **butter**
1	cup	shredded **dried coconut**
1	large	**egg**

Blueberry Crumb Bars

3½ cups **Essential Eating Sprouted Flour**
1 cup **maple sugar**
1 teaspoon **cinnamon**
¼ teaspoon **nutmeg**
¼ teaspoon **sea salt**
½ cup **butter**
2 tablespoons **butter**
1½ teaspoons **baking powder**
½ teaspoon **baking soda**
1½ cups **yogurt** or sour cream
2 large **eggs**
½ cup **agave nectar**
1 teaspoon **vanilla**
½ teaspoon grated **lemon rind**
3 cups fresh **blueberries**

Preheat the oven to 350°F. Combine the first 5 ingredients in a large bowl. Cut in the ½ cup of butter with a pastry blender until the mixture resembles coarse meal. Place 1 cup of the flour mixture in a small bowl and cut in the remaining 2 tablespoons of butter to make a streusel; set aside. Add the baking powder and baking soda to the remaining flour mixture and stir well. Combine the yogurt or sour cream, eggs, agave nectar, vanilla and lemon rind. Pour the wet ingredients over the flour mixture and beat with an electric mixer on low speed until well blended. Pour the batter into a 13- by 9-inch greased baking pan. Top the batter with the blueberries, and sprinkle with the reserved streusel. Bake approximately 45 minutes, or until a wooden toothpick inserted in the center of the cake comes out clean. Allow the cake to cool on a wire rack.

Pancakes and Waffles

Sunrise Pancakes

1	large **egg**
1½	cups **yogurt**
2	tablespoons **maple syrup**
1	cup **Essential Eating Sprouted Flour**
½	teaspoon **sea salt**
½	teaspoon **baking soda**
2	teaspoons **baking powder**
¼	cup **cornmeal**
1	tablespoon **poppy seeds** (optional)

In a medium bowl, mix all the ingredients together until blended. Pour ¼ cup of batter onto a hot, greased griddle or cast-iron skillet until bubbles begin to form on top; flip, and continue to cook until done. Serve with butter and maple syrup.

Wild Rice Pancakes

In a large bowl, mix the dry ingredients. In another bowl, whisk together the yogurt, wild rice, butter and eggs. Add the wet ingredients to the dry ingredients, stirring until just combined and being careful not to overmix. The batter will be thick and slightly lumpy. Heat a griddle or cast-iron skillet over medium heat for 3–4 minutes, then lightly grease with ghee. Using a ¹/₄-cup measure for each pancake, pour the batter onto the griddle or skillet. Cook until bubbles surface, about 2 minutes. Flip the pancake only once. The second side will take about 1 minute to cook.

1	cup **Essential Eating Sprouted Flour**
2	teaspoons **baking powder**
½	teaspoon **baking soda**
¼	teaspoon **sea salt**
1	cup **yogurt**
½	cup cooked **wild rice**, cooled
2	tablespoons **butter**, melted
2	large **eggs**

Pancakes and Waffles

Quinoa Flake Pancakes

Makes 12 pancakes.

1	cup **Essential Eating Sprouted Flour**
1	cup **quinoa flakes**
1	tablespoon **baking powder**
½	teaspoon **sea salt**
1	large **egg**
3	tablespoons **butter**, melted
1¼	cups **water**
¼	cup **yogurt**

In a medium bowl, mix the flour, quinoa flakes, baking powder and salt. In a separate bowl, whisk the egg and butter; mix in the water and yogurt. Add the liquid mixture to the flour mixture; mix just until blended. Preheat a skillet or griddle. Pour ¼ cup of batter per pancake onto the griddle. Cook until bubbles begin to form on top; flip, and continue to cook until done. Serve with butter and maple syrup.

Tapioca Waffles

2 large **eggs**

¼ cup **yogurt**

1¼ cups **water**

3 tablespoons **butter**, melted

¼ cup **maple syrup**

1 tablespoon **vanilla**

1½ cups **Essential Eating Sprouted Flour**

½ cup **tapioca flour**

½ teaspoon **sea salt**

1 teaspoon **baking powder**

In a large mixing bowl, lightly beat the eggs. Add the yogurt, water, butter, syrup and vanilla. Mix until smooth. Add the remaining dry ingredients to the egg mixture and mix until blended. Follow the waffle iron instructions for cooking. Adjust the consistency of the batter by adding more water or flour as needed. Serve with butter and maple syrup.

Blueberry Corn Waffles

2   large **eggs**
½   cup **yogurt**
1   cup **water**
3   tablespoons **butter**, melted
¼   cup **agave nectar** or maple syrup
1   tablespoon **vanilla**
1   cup **Essential Eating Sprouted Flour**
¾   cup **corn flour**
½   teaspoon **sea salt**
1   teaspoon **baking powder**
1   cup fresh or frozen **blueberries**

In a large mixing bowl, lightly beat the eggs. Add the yogurt, water, butter, agave nectar or maple syrup and vanilla. Mix until smooth. Add the remaining dry ingredients to the egg mixture, stir in the blueberries and mix until blended. Follow the waffle iron instructions for cooking. Adjust the consistency of the batter by adding more water or flour as needed. Serve with butter and maple syrup.

Coconut Waffles

Makes 4 servings.

2	large **eggs**
¼	cup **yogurt**
1 ¼	cups **water**
3	tablespoons **coconut oil**
¼	cup **maple syrup**
1	tablespoon **vanilla extract**
1 ¼	cups **Essential Eating Sprouted Flour**
½	cup **coconut flour**
½	teaspoon **sea salt**
1	teaspoon **baking powder**
4	tablespoons dried, shredded **coconut**

In a large mixing bowl, lightly beat the eggs. Add the yogurt, water, oil, syrup and vanilla. Mix until blended. Add the remaining dry ingredients to the egg mixture and mix until blended. Follow the waffle iron instructions for cooking. Adjust the consistency of the batter by adding more water or flour as needed. Serve with butter and maple syrup.

Pizza, Pasta and Flatbread

Vegetable Pizza

1⅛ cups **water**

3 tablespoons **olive oil**

3 cups **Essential Eating Sprouted Flour**

1½ teaspoons **sea salt**

1½ teaspoons **maple sugar**

1½ teaspoons **yeast**

SUGGESTED TOPPINGS:

1 cup **pizza sauce**

2 cups **spinach**, cooked and chopped

4 **scallions**, chopped

8 ounces sliced **mushrooms**

¼ cup **sun-dried tomatoes**, reconstituted

¼ cup **black olives**

2 teaspoons dried **sweet basil**

2 teaspoons dried **oregano**

1 teaspoon **Herbamare**

½ teaspoon **pepper**

½ cup **Yogurt Cheese**, drop by teaspoonfuls on top

1 tablespoon **paprika**, sprinkled on top

Preheat the oven to 500°F.

To make the dough by hand, place the pizza dough ingredients in a large bowl and mix well. Remove the dough from the bowl and knead it into a ball. Coat the bowl with olive oil; place the dough back in the bowl and turn it once to coat with oil. Cover the bowl with a clean dish towel and let it stand for 30 minutes, or until the dough doubles in size. Roll out the dough to the desired size. Place it on a greased baking pan and add the desired toppings. Bake 8–12 minutes. A pizza stone may also be used. Preheat the stone; slide the pizza onto the stone with a pizza peel and bake as above.

To make the dough in a bread machine, place the pizza dough ingredients in the baking pan of the machine in the order listed. Program the machine for pizza dough and press start. Remove the dough from the machine; roll the dough out to the desired size and bake as above.

Herbed Crust Pizza

*Makes one 15-inch thick
or two thin pizzas.*

Preheat the oven to 500°F.

To make by hand, place the pizza dough ingredients in a large bowl and mix well. Remove the dough from the bowl and knead it into a ball. Coat the bowl with olive oil; place the dough back in the bowl and turn it once to coat with oil. Cover the bowl with a clean dish towel and let it stand for 30 minutes, or until the dough doubles in size. Roll out the dough to the desired size. Place it on a greased baking pan and add the toppings. Bake 8–12 minutes. Alternatively, a pizza stone may be used. Preheat the stone, slide the pizza onto the stone with a pizza peel and bake as above.

To make dough in a bread machine, place the ingredients in the baking pan of the machine in the order listed. Program the machine for pizza dough and press start. Remove the dough from the machine; roll the dough out to the desired size and bake as above.

1 ⅛ cups **water**
3 tablespoons **olive oil**
3 cups **Essential Eating Sprouted Flour**
1 ½ teaspoons **sea salt**
1 ½ teaspoons **maple sugar**
1 ½ teaspoons **yeast**
2 tablespoons dried **herbs**, such as sweet basil, oregano, thyme or rosemary

SUGGESTED TOPPINGS:
1 cup **pizza sauce**
4 **scallions**, sliced
2–3 cups **roasted veggies** such as eggplant, zucchini and tomatoes
2 tablespoons fresh **parsley**
1 teaspoon **Herbamare**
½ teaspoon **pepper**
½ cup **Yogurt Cheese**, drop by teaspoonfuls on top
1 tablespoon **paprika**, sprinkled on top

Pizza, Pasta and Flatbread

Roasted Tomato Basil Ravioli

Makes 6 servings.

FOR FILLING:

8–10 medium (about 3 cups) **tomatoes**, coarsely chopped, or one 28-ounce can whole tomatoes, drained

2 medium **onions**, coarsely chopped

12 **basil leaves**, cut into slivers

Herbamare and **pepper** to taste

PASTA:

3½–4 cups **Essential Eating Sprouted Flour**

5 large **eggs**

2 teaspoons **olive oil**

1 teaspoon **sea salt**

Preheat the oven to 375°F. To make the filling, combine the ingredients on a jellyroll pan and place in the oven. Roast for 1½ hours, stirring occasionally as the liquid reduces and the vegetables soften. Let the filling cool on the pan while the pasta dough is prepared. The mixture may also be slow-roasted at 250°F for 3–4 hours.

To make the pasta, combine 1 cup of the flour and the remaining dough ingredients in the large bowl of a stand mixer; mix on low for 2 minutes. Stir in enough of the remaining flour to make a soft dough; remove it from the bowl and knead it until it is smooth and not sticky, about 10 minutes, adding more flour as needed. The dough may also be mixed by hand. Wrap the dough in waxed paper and let it rest for 30 minutes.

Put a large pot of water on the stovetop to boil. Separate the dough into two pieces. Keep the unused portion covered with a cloth. On a floured surface, roll out the dough from the middle, flipping it occasionally and flouring it as necessary to keep it from sticking. Keep flipping and rolling it into a thin sheet. Cut it into manageable lengths, if necessary. Cover it with a cloth and roll out the remaining portion of the dough. When the second sheet has been rolled out, place one rounded tablespoonful of the filling equally spaced 2¼ inches apart. Using a pastry brush, lightly coat the spaces between the filling portions with water in preparation for sealing the edges of the dough. Gently lay the first rolled sheet of pasta on top, matching up the sheets evenly. Using your fingertips, press out any air bubbles surrounding the filling. Using a sharp knife or a pastry wheel, cut the pasta into $2^1/_4$-inch squares. To crimp the edges of the ravioli, gently press them with the tines of a fork. In a pot of boiling water, cook the pasta 3–5 minutes, until al dente. Drain and drizzle with olive oil and sprinkle with fresh parsley.

Linguini with Tomatoes and Herbs

Makes 4 servings.

In the large bowl of a stand mixer, combine 1 cup of the flour and the remaining dough ingredients; mix on low for 2 minutes. Stir in enough of the remaining flour to make a soft dough; remove it from the bowl and knead it until it is smooth and not sticky, about 10 minutes, adding more flour as needed. The dough may also be mixed by hand. Wrap the dough in waxed paper and let it rest for 30 minutes.

Work with half the dough at a time, and keep the other half covered. On a lightly floured surface, roll the dough into a rectangle ⅛ inch thick. Cut the dough lengthwise in ⅜-inch-wide strips and let the strips air-dry on a cloth for 15 minutes before cooking. Roll out and cut the remaining dough. Bring a stockpot of water to a boil. Add 2 tablespoons oil and 1 teaspoon salt to the boiling water. Gently place the pasta in the boiling water and cook until al dente, 2–5 minutes. Drain and top with the remaining ingredients.

PASTA:
- 3½–4 cups **Essential Eating Sprouted Flour**
- 5 large **eggs**
- 2 teaspoons **olive oil**
- 1 teaspoon **sea salt**

TOPPING:
- 2 cups fresh **tomatoes**, chopped
- 4 tablespoons fresh **parsley**, chopped
- 4 tablespoons fresh **chives**, snipped
  Cold-pressed, **extra-virgin olive oil**, drizzled on top
  Sea salt and **pepper** to taste

∽◡ **NOTE:** 1¼ cups of water may be substituted for the eggs. For green pasta, add ½ cup cooked, squeezed-dry, finely chopped spinach with the flour.

Herbed Focaccia

4½ cups **Essential Eating Sprouted Flour**
1½ cups lukewarm **water**
1½ teaspoons **yeast**
1 teaspoon **sea salt**
2 tablespoons fresh **rosemary** or thyme, chopped, plus extra for sprinkling
2 tablespoons **olive oil**

TOPPING:
3 tablespoons **olive oil**
1 tablespoon coarse **sea salt**

Place the flour in a large bowl and form a deep well in the center. Pour the water into the well, sprinkle with the yeast and let soften 5 minutes. Using the fingers of one hand, gently combine part of the flour with the water to make a soupy paste without going to the bottom of the bowl. Cover it with a kitchen towel and let it rise in a warm place for 30 minutes, or until bubbles form at the surface.

Add the salt, herbs and oil. Using one hand, mix the ingredients in the bowl to incorporate the rest of the flour until the dough forms a sticky ball. Turn out the dough onto a lightly floured surface; knead 8–10 minutes until smooth. A stand mixer fitted with a dough hook may be used. The dough will be sticky, which results in a light-textured flatbread. Place the dough in an oiled bowl, cover it and let it rise in a warm place until double, about 1½ hours.

Twenty minutes prior to the dough being ready, preheat the oven to 450°F. Grease a baking sheet with ghee or olive oil. Working lightly, use a rolling pin or shape the dough with your hands to fit the pan. Cover it with a cloth and let it rise in a warm place until double, about 20 minutes. Brush the dough with olive oil and sprinkle with coarse salt. Oil your fingertips and make indentations about 1/2 inch deep and 1 inch apart all over the top of the dough. Bake 25–30 minutes, until golden brown. Remove from the oven and transfer the flatbread to a wire rack to cool.

Sources

After years of baking and writing about real foods, I've prepared the following list of some of my favorite food companies, products and equipment that can be found in local stores and online. Although many of these companies carry a larger variety of food items, only the items that are used in these recipes are listed.

Fruits, Veggies, Miscellaneous Flours and Food Items

ARROWHEAD MILLS
Box 2059
Hereford, TX 79045
806-364-0730 / Fax 806-364-8242
Organic quinoa, quinoa flakes, quinoa flour, organic cornmeal (blue, high-lysine, yellow and white)

BOB'S RED MILL NATURAL FOODS
5209 SE International Way
Milwaukee, OR 97222
800-553-2258 or 503-654-3215
Fax 503-653-1339
www.bobsredmill.com
Corn flour, coconut flour

Sprouted Baked Goods

BERKSHIRE MOUNTAIN BAKERY, INC.
367 Park Street, Route 183
Housatonic, MA 01236
413-274-3412
info@berkshiremountainbakery.com
www.berkshiremountainbakery.com
Sprouted whole grain spelt cookies

DOROTHY LANE MARKETS
Oakwood, Washington Square and Springboro, OH
800-824-1294
Email dlm@dorothylane.com
www.DorothyLane.com
Freshly baked organic sprouted bread, rolls, cookies and pizza crust

UNIQUE PRETZEL BAKERY, INC.
215 E. Bellevue Avenue
Reading, PA 19605
888-477-5487
Unique Essential Eating Sprouted Pretzel Splits available at your local store or shipped anywhere

WEGMANS FOOD MARKETS
1500 Brooks Avenue
P.O. Box 30844
Rochester, NY 14603-0844
1-800-WEGMANS
www.Wegmans.com
Over 70 stores located throughout New York, New Jersey Pennsylvania, Maryland and Virginia, introducing freshly baked organic sprouted bread

Sprouted Flours

ESSENTIAL EATING SPROUTED FOODS
P.O. Box 216
Mifflinville, PA 18631
570-586-1557 / Fax 570-586-3112
Email info@EssentialEating.com
www.EssentialEating.com
Certified organic sprouted whole wheat and whole spelt flours in bulk

SHILOH FARMS
191 Commerce Drive
New Holland, PA 17557
800–362-6832
Email info@shilohfarms.net
www.shilohfarms.com
Distributes 2-, 5- and 30-pound bags in case lots of Shiloh Farms Essential Eating Sprouted Whole Wheat and Sprouted Whole Spelt flours. Available direct or through health food stores. Sprouted whole grain spelt flour baking mixes.

BASCOM MAPLE FARMS, INC.
Box 137, Alstead, NH 03602
800-835-6361
Maple syrup and sugar

BUTTERNUT MOUNTAIN FARM
37 Industrial Park Drive
Morrisville, VT 05661
800-828–2376 / Fax 802-888-5909
Maple syrup, sugar and cream

COOMBS VERMONT GOURMET
Box 186
Jacksonville, VT 05342-0186
888-266-6271 or 802-368-2513
Fax 802–368–2516
Email vtmaple@sover.net
Maple syrup

HIGHLAND SUGARWORKS, INC.
Box 58, Wilson Industrial Park
Websterville, VT 05678-0058
802-479-1747 / Fax 802-479-1737
www.highlandsugarworks.com
Maple syrup, maple sugar and maple butter/cream

SHADY MAPLE FARM, LTD.
786 8th Street E.
La Guadeloupe, PQ G0M 1G0, Canada
800-493-5844 or 418-459-6161
Fax 418-459-6788
Email shady@quebectel.com
www.shadymaple.com
Maple syrup

WHOLESOME SWEETENERS, INC.
8016 Highway 90-A
Sugar Land, TX 77478
800-680-1896
Email info@wholesomesweeteners.com
www.wholesomesweeteners.com
Organic raw agave nectar

Herbs, Spices, Vanilla and Yeast

THE BAKER'S CATALOG
P.O. Box 876
Norwich, VT 05055-0876
800-827-6836
Herbs, yeast, sea salt and vanilla

CELTIC SEA SALT
800-867-7258
Email info@celtic-seasalt.com
www.celticseasalt.com
Sea salt and agave nectar

FRONTIER COOPERATIVE HERBS
Box 299
Norway, IA 52318-0299
800-669-3275 or 319-227-7996
Fax 319-227-7966
Email info@frontierherb.com
www.frontierherb.com
*Frontier Herbs and Simply Organic Spices, organic
vanilla, organic carob powder*

RAPUNZEL
260 Lake Road
Dayville, CT 06241
Email custservrapunzel@unfi.com
*Organic yeast, A-Vogel Herbamare® and
Trocomare® seasoning sea salts.*

REAL SALT
Redmond Minerals, Inc.
Redmond, UT 84562
800-367-7258
Real, unprocessed mineral table salt

RED STAR YEAST PRODUCTS
Universal Food Corporation
433 E. Michigan Street
Milwaukee, WI 53202
800-558-9892 or 414-347-3832
Fax 414-347-4789
www.redstaryeast.com
Active dry baking yeast

Baking Products and Equipment

THE BAKER'S CATALOG
P. O. Box 876
Norwich, VT 05055-0876
800-827-6836
Baking equipment, bread machines and Donvier®
Wave Yogurt Strainer; catalog

DONVIER WHITE WAVE YOGURT STRAINER
www.cooking.com
www.epinions.com
Online stores for yogurt cheese strainer

HEALTHWISE
13659 Victory Blvd.
Van Nuys, CA 91401
800-942-3262
Bread machines

NATURAL VALUE
14 Waterthrush Court
Sacramento, CA 95831
916-427-7242 / Fax 916-427-3784
www.naturalvalue.com
Waxed paper sandwich bags, natural cleaning
sponges, cloths, scour pads and recycled trash bags,
available at health food stores

N.E.E.D.S. (NUTRITIONAL ECOLOGY ENVIRONMENTAL DELIVERY SYSTEM)
P.O. Box 580
East Syracuse, NY 13057
800-634-1380 / Fax 800-295-NEED
Email needs@needs.com / www.needs.com
Health and wellness mail-order catalog offers
cellophane bags for safe food storage

SEVENTH GENERATION, INC.
212 Battery Street, Suite A
Burlington, VT 05401-5281
800-456-1191
www.seventhgen.com
Selection of detergents and cleansers that are
nontoxic, biodegradable and free of perfumes and
dyes; recycled and recyclable paper towels and napkins

WILLIAMS-SONOMA
Box 7456
San Francisco, CA 94120-7456
800-541-2233
www.williams-sonoma.com
Cast-iron pizza pan with handles; catalog

Epilogue:
The Destiny of a Seed

The destiny of a seed, as Mother Nature designed it, is to sprout. Seeds or grains travel unsprouted through the digestive tract waiting for an environment in which they can fulfill their destiny—a destiny that allows the seed to burst into an alive food. It is impossible for a seed to fulfill its destiny inside the human body, because the digestive process prevents the seed from sprouting. Like a caterpillar becoming a butterfly, sprouting is a natural metamorphosis in the cycle of life.

An animal pasture, in the summertime, is excellent proof that a seed cannot break down or sprout in the digestive tract. Whole seeds eaten by animals, but not crushed by chewing, sprout easily once they reach an environment that is conducive to germination such as an "organic" compost pile. The seeds fulfill their destiny in the "pasture patties" that the animals excrete, not in the animals' digestive tracts.

When grains sprout and are milled into flour, they have fulfilled their destiny prior to entering your digestive tract. The grain in its sprouted form is a live plant bursting with vital nutrients—nutrients that are now ready to nourish, not merely pass through, your body. A sprouted seed is so much easier for your body to assimilate and also less likely to cause you indigestion. As we strive to replace the overly processed foods in our diets with real food, I find it astonishing how sprouts fulfill their destiny in preparation for supporting our health. As the seed achieves its goal of sprouting, we, as Essential Eaters, fulfill our goals to eat and digest real food as well. Go forth and sprout!

Compost Matters

Compost is nature's way of recycling. Before human intervention, all organic materials on earth were completely composted and recycled back into the earth. Although there is an entire industry built around composting, it can be as easy as burying your kitchen scraps in a hole dug in the ground, where they can decompose. Compost replenishes necessary nutrients in a balanced way that authentically improves the quality and health of soil.

Organic materials such as kitchen scraps and yard waste account for one-third of our household trash, which could easily be kept out of landfills and, in turn, enrich our soil. Composting can be fun and rewarding, even for those who do not garden. Compost piles, even the most inefficient ones, rarely get filled up, because they just continue to decompose. Consider composting. It takes little effort and produces such fertile results. Compost matters.

Composting is a process of transformation, just like writing a book. With the passing of time, nature turns a pail of kitchen scraps into rich, black gold in the form of aromatic earth, creating a usable result, just as writing transforms thoughts into meaningful words and healthy recipes. The serendipity of writing parallels the composting process.

With deep gratitude, I thank the following group of talented individuals who have shared in the transformation process to create this book. Without them, my compost would be just a pile of kitchen scraps. With love to my husband, Tony, and to Katherine Acevedo, Tony Acquaviva, Georgia Anderson, Damien Blanchard, Richard Brandt, Bill Carrington, Ginny Carroll, Lee Ann Cavanaugh, Kate Collins, Jim Dunleavy, Peter Eckman, Yvonne Eckman, Rebecca Gillette, Matthew Kelly, Valerie Kiser, Kathryn Lesoine, Donna McDonald, Linda Madoff, Eluka Moore, Tracy Pitz, Rick Rippon, Nancy Rosolino, Beth Schulefand, Cindy Szili and Nancy Trauger. I am deeply grateful for your many talents and sustaining support.

Index